Claudel on the Theatre

PAUL CLAUDEL

Claudel
on the Theatre

EDITED BY
JACQUES PETIT AND JEAN-PIERRE KEMPF
TRANSLATED BY
CHRISTINE TROLLOPE

UNIVERSITY OF MIAMI PRESS
Coral Gables, Florida

Originally published as
Mes idées sur le Théâtre
© Éditions Gallimard 1966
This translation copyright © 1972
by University of Miami Press
Library of Congress Catalog Card No. 76–121683
ISBN 0–87024–158–3

Manufactured in the United States of America

Contents

vi / Contents

Illustrations

Translator's Note

As far as the material in this book is concerned, I have followed the editors exactly, leaving out what they left out. The translation itself was not such a simple matter. Claudel is not an easy writer to interpret. He thinks his own thoughts, expresses them in his own words, and his words are not always the ones we might expect. To Paul Claudel a word means what he wants it to mean and nothing else. Hence his frequent obscurities.

I have translated as literally as I could, and chosen my English words as carefully as Claudel chose his French ones. But I could not always be literal. There were times when I had to reach into Claudel's mind, to "tune in," as it were, to his thought processes, before I could understand what he really meant. On such occasions I have had to take liberties and translate the essence rather than the words. But I have done my best to keep the flavor of the original, the delicate precision of phrase, the occasional sentence left in midair, the artificial, almost rococo, ornamentation, and the subtle rhythms that betray his passion for music.

Christine Trollope

Preface

      Claudel's passionate interest in the technical problems of the theatre goes back a long way, to the first production of one of his plays, *L'Annonce faite à Marie,* at the Théâtre de l'Oeuvre in 1912. Even before that date he had sometimes thought deeply about the theatre, when rewriting his first plays or when, in *L'Échange,* he created the character of the actress Lechy Elbernon. His interest in the Chinese theatre was that of a technician as much as a poet. After seeing some performances of Wagner in Vienna, he made a few notes about the sets. By going to rehearsals in 1912 he learned something of the work of producers and actors. He was not at all put off by the discipline of the theatre, and watched with eager curiosity his own words gradually coming to life. "It is really fascinating," he wrote to André Gide, "to work on a piece of business, a movement or a grouping, and to see it all taking shape."

      This lively interest stayed with Claudel all his life. He was always deeply concerned with the interpretation of his work; he liked to have his say in the production, was lavish with advice to the actors, and often made elaborate plans for performances which never took place. He had at the same time a more general interest in the theatre. His curiosity was insatiable, he watched carefully what was going on—and he worked on the problems by himself. There is thus plenty of material to be found in his letters and writings; we had to select the most representative passages and arrange them in some kind of order.

      The simplest arrangement seemed to be chronological, and the stages in the development of Claudel's ideas are at once apparent. First, vague dreams about the theatre glimpsed in his first plays, a few letters, and a poem. This first period ends in 1912. Then begin the years of "apprenticeship" with lessons picked up haphazardly by working with

Lugné-Poe, Alexandre de Salzmann, Jaques-Dalcroze and Jacques Copeau, and from chance meetings and discoveries. He was captivated by the experiments at Hellerau, seeing in them a complete rebirth of the art of the theatre, and he tried in vain to get his French colleagues to share his enthusiasm. The art of the ballet was revealed to him by Nijinsky in Brazil, and the Japanese theatre in all its forms—Nō, Kabuki, Bugaku, Bunraku—gave him endless food for thought. This is not, however, so much a matter of influence as of recognition. Claudel was seeing his dreams become reality; rather than discovering new ideas, he was confirming those he already had. Even when he had finished *Le Soulier de satin*—which, of all his plays, is the one that shows all these preoccupations most clearly—his interest in the theatre continued. In fact, he became even more immersed in it. Having worked out his technique to his own satisfaction, he was able to view it with detachment and was ready to accede without too much reluctance to the entreaties of Philippe Berthelot, Max Reinhardt, and Ida Rubinstein. This marked the beginning of a period of experimental drama that ended much later with *Le Ravissement de Scapin. Sous le rempart d'Athènes, Le Livre de Christophe Colomb, Le Festin de la sagesse*, and *L'Histoire de Tobie et de Sara* can all be called "experiments" without making them appear any less valuable and significant. Each of them gave the poet an opportunity for technical research, and each was a solution to one particular problem. He was always willing to provide his own commentary; "Drama and Music" was written to explain *Le Livre de Christophe Colomb*, and *Le Festin de la sagesse* was introduced by "An Experiment in the Adaptation of the Japanese Nō Drama." After the war his work at last received a hearing. His dreams had to give way to material considerations, but he did at least manage to translate some of them into reality.

We have arranged the texts in this particular order to show Claudel's development and to emphasize the variety of his ideas. But there are of course certain constants which have to be defined. Some are easily seen: there are themes which recur from one text to the other, representing theories which Claudel stubbornly refused to give up. From the very beginning, for instance, he paid careful attention to minute details of diction and gesture, and his attitude was so high-handed as to be a constant source of embarrassment to both actors and audience. But there are also contradictions, showing that the poet's vision and tastes were by no means immutable.

Claudel has nothing that could be called a dramatic system. We have been able to establish the general direction of his opinions, but nothing definite enough to enable us to arrange his writings into a treatise on dramatic art. As we have already said, and will certainly say again, he makes a few basic demands, but the interest of his writings as a whole lies in the picture they give us of a fertile imagination at grips with the techniques and problems of the theatre. We see in them his absolute conviction that "creation" does not stop with the publication of a work, and that production does not merely interpret a play but—as he wrote to Pottecher as early as 1897—completes it, gives it an outward form. Later he said that "ideas borrow from art and at the same time give art the power to clothe ideas in words." This means that the poet should collaborate closely in the production so that it can restore to him in full measure what he has given to it. A performance is creative or, rather, recreative. Claudel never attended rehearsals of his plays merely to make sure that his text was being faithfully interpreted; his purpose was to follow the development of the play with and through the actors. He never saw such work as cutting, revising, and rearranging as an irritating subjection to external pressures, but as a new and faithful source of inspiration. He may have grumbled at the time, but seldom failed to express satisfaction later. Very early, before he had had any experience in the theatre, he said "Art has no final solution," and he never changed his mind. In his opinion, everything could be taken apart and put together again. His adaptability invariably exasperated his producer; the moment came when, as Jean-Louis Barrault said, the thing must be "set," and then Claudel would start revising all over again.

Imagination, as he suggested so admirably in *La Légende de Prakriti*, enriches itself unceasingly. The slightest notion grows until it reaches grandiose dimensions; ideas spring one from another, accumulate, and destroy each other. For example, he would design a set and, as he said of Prakriti, he had scarcely submitted it when he thought of a better one. He asked Darius Milhaud for some musical arrangements for *L'Annonce faite à Marie* and went on dreaming about it to such an extent that a few days later he suggested turning the whole play into an opera. He had a chance to put on *Protée*, immediately gave full rein to his imagination, and thought out a set, then two, then three, with costumes and even stage business. And so he went on, revising, changing, polishing. It was inevitable that any actual performance must disappoint him to a greater or lesser extent. He had already gone beyond it and had much better ideas as to how the play should be staged.

Closely bound up with this expansiveness, this upsurge of creative force, is a dream that is perhaps the focal point of all his work on theatrical technique—that of "total theatre," in which the poet calls upon the services not only of the scenic designer, the producer, and the actor, but also of the dancer, the composer, and the film-maker. Words are not enough; at certain points they need the support of music, and then the music turns to singing and calls for movement, and movement becomes dancing; and then sometimes the very presence of the actors is too immediate, and only film can give the play what it needs. All these various elements are brought in, not to delight the audience, but to give the text all the emotional power of which it is capable. All Claudel's experiments—ballets, mime, oratorios, operas, films—are thus explained. He neglected not one of the possible resources of the theatre, but endeavored to place them all in subjection to his poetry, so that this "total theatre" would in fact be simply the natural emanation of the text.

We see from notes in his journal that the first problem Claudel tackled, even before he had seen any of his plays performed, was that of the set. His taste at that time appears to have tended toward realism. The scene, he said, should be three-dimensional, optical illusions should be avoided, and colors should be as true as possible. With an odd attention to detail he insisted that "completely new clothes" should not be used. And in fact at the Théâtre de l'Oeuvre in 1902 and at Hellerau in 1913 he accepted with enthusiasm an almost nonexistent setting for *L'Annonce faite à Marie*. The lighting on the stage of the Salle Malakoff concealed its poverty and gave the illusion of a change of set. At Hellerau it played an even more important part; in fact, as he said himself, it did everything. He went so far as to assert that all his plays would henceforth be staged in this way. In Germany he particularly liked the stage on different levels—about as far from realism as it is possible to get—because of the symbolism it allowed. Characters appeared at different heights, according to their circumstances; at the lowest level by the hearth, in the center where the table was placed, or at the top where there was a door. He appears to have been directly responsible for this set. He immediately constructed round it a "theory" which does not appear explicitly anywhere else—that of "permanent actors" (here, the hearth, the table, and the door) and thought that in so doing he had rediscovered the staging of the old mystery plays. He never lost his conviction that the scene should be symbolic rather than functional—not a mere background for the actors, but a projection of the text itself, stressing and clarifying the poet's meaning. Thus in

Partage de midi he set great store by the omega shape that closes around the two protagonists, from the Chinese tomb in the second act to the armchair in the last. For that reason he incorporated in the final version of *L'Échange*, in an almost identical form, the hammock thought up by Copeau for Louis Laine; he turned it into a swing—a "permanent actor" in the play—which allows all sorts of symbolic business. He expressed very similar ideas with regard to the sets for *Le Soulier de satin*, and when reviewing the Old Vic's production of *King Lear*, he said it was a pity that the similar reaction of the two sisters had not been suggested by symmetry in the sets. We have then a fairly clear picture of Claudel's opinions on this particular point.

But we are met at once by obvious contradictions. He still had the same passion for realism. A tree is a hard cylindrical object. A door is meant to open and close and parted curtains are not the same thing at all. He continued to reject anything fake or illusory, or even stylized, and to worry about tiny details like the length of Turelure's side-whiskers in *L'Otage*, and the color of the Pope's girdle. His contradictions do not appear one after the other, but all at once, as shown in the demands he made on Lugné-Poe. Similarly, at the very moment when, full of enthusiasm for Hellerau, he was declaring that his next plays "will need no scenery and can be acted anywhere," he began to write *Le Pain dur*, with a minutely described and completely realistic set. The other inconsistency is that he never lost his taste for spectacular sets, often baroque in style. He wavered between simplicity and excessive elaboration, going constantly from one extreme to the other. For *L'Annonce faite à Marie* he advised a producer to have no scenery at all and a few days later sent him photographs of stained-glass windows and a cathedral porch to give him ideas. He said he had written *Protée* to be played on the stage at Hellerau and a few years later he worked out a most ingenious and elaborate set for the same play. There are two completely different sets for *L'Annonce*, dating from 1912 and 1955. Jean Variot, who designed the first of them, rightly noted that both were deliberately chosen by Claudel. His feeling for the baroque—in the strictest sense of the word—finally took him beyond even this exuberance, and he began to envisage a changing, shifting background which, as he clearly states with regard to *L'Histoire de Tobie et de Sara*, the cinema could provide.

His views on production show the same contraditions, but his ideas on acting are more stable and his demands more definite. There is little difference between the notes he made for the Théâtre de l'Oeuvre company in 1912 and those he wrote at the end of his life; the later ones contain some more precise details, but the point of view is the same. We have nothing to add to the detailed study which has already been made of these ideas,* and the notes themselves are clear and concise. Claudel wished to impose on his actors a style of speaking that would bring out the musical qualities of his verse, in opposition to the critics who accused the actors of "intoning," and perhaps a little in opposition to the actors themselves. He also insisted—which was less easy—that gesture should never be gesticulation or even the actor's own natural expression, but that the actor too should see it as the projection and completion of the words. His views on this subject later became rather advanced.

On seeing the experiments of Jaques-Dalcroze in 1913, he was struck by the sculptural beauty of which gesture was capable, and emphasized this in his articles on Hellerau. It fell to Nijinsky to give him an even better insight into the powers of expression of the body. Claudel wrote for him *L'Homme et son désir*, which is much more than a ballet. As we have tried to show by a comparison of texts, it is an attempt to express a poetic image in plastic form. He learned from watching Japanese Nō plays that gestures gain a deeper significance by being slow and grave. This solemnity gives them their full measure of emotion—we could even say of poetry, for Claudel explains his point by means of analogies from poetry. In both Nō drama and the dancing of Nijinsky, everyday actions are given their true significance, exactly as happens in poetry to everyday words and familiar images. He said of the Japanese actors, "Now we can understand how every one of our poor random gestures was the unconscious imitation of some eternal attitude," and of Nijinsky he wrote, "He takes our most misusual gestures, as Virgil took our words and images, and transports them into the blissful realm of all that is intelligent, powerful, and ethereal"—in short into the world of art, and of poetry, of which Virgil is for him the most perfect expression. Later, in *Le Jet de pierre*, he attempted to write "plastic poems" which we might call "exercises"—a series of everyday movements and gestures that have to be brought to perfection. The most important outcome of this research consists in the mime plays and those works in which gesture supported by music is so important, such as *Le Livre de Christophe Colomb* or *Jeanne d'Arc au bûcher*. The latter, he tells us, was even inspired by a gesture.

* See Rene Farabet, *Le Jeu de l'Acteur dans le theatre de Paul Claudel*, Lettres modernes, 1960.

While considering gesture, Claudel was following a parallel, but richer, train of thought in music, springing naturally from his ideas on diction and on poetry as he longed to hear it spoken by actors. The first idea along these lines, which he submitted to Darius Milhaud as early as 1913, was the transition from words to music, or, putting it more exactly, "the attempt to weld together words and music." He made his first experiments with the trilogy of Aeschylus: "We need something like the note on which the Epistles and the Gospels are chanted, which can turn into true song without a break." Music would thus play different parts, sometimes supporting the rhythm, sometimes imposing it, and sometimes helping speech to rise until it becomes song. It would lose its independence and be subordinated to poetry or, rather, born of it. Music "in the process of birth" is an expression often used by Claudel. The ideal, he says, would be for music to spring "from poetry, as poetry springs from prose, and prose from silence and the formless mutterings of the mind." Here again we see his dream of "total art." Music would extend and complete poetry, saying what cannot be expressed by words alone.

His thoughts on music led to other, less ambitious ideas. He felt very strongly the need for music as a support for at least certain scenes in his plays, sometimes for the whole play. Writing about *Jeanne d'Arc au bûcher,* he showed the value of its contribution very clearly: "It intensifies the rhythm, opens the heart, in the same way as the chord spreads to every passion, impregnates speech with feeling and thought, and both speaks and listens at the same time." The notion that music "intensifies the rhythm," "impregnates speech with feeling," and creates an atmosphere is all rather banal. But it led to interesting experiments such as the one he conducted with Darius Milhaud, who attempted to create a musical accompaniment to *L'Annonce faite à Marie* as a kind of commentary, a reflection of the action. The music for which Claudel asked was "muffled, like the countryside breathing." The last idea is the most important. It appears to have been suggested by the Japanese theatre, but is already mentioned in a prose poem, "Théâtre," in *Connaissance de l'est.* Music, he says, can play the part of the chorus, express the feelings of the audience, and reply to the action. In fact, music "listens."

His researches, presented like this, appear more systematic than they really were, but at least in these two fields Claudel showed stubbornness and perseverance. His attitude toward technical problems gave more consideration to imagination or even fantasy. We find in his writings several odd ideas and original "discoveries," but we would not go so far as to call them inventions in the strict sense. Claudel was not, for example, the first to advocate the use of film in production. He simply tried to bring a few new ideas into the theory of acting. For example, he suggested duplicating the actors in certain cases, each followed by another exactly like him, as if by a shadow. This idea was used in *Sous le rempart d'Athènes*, and Claudel would have liked to use it again for *L'Annonce faite à Marie*. As the second actor did not speak, the intention seemed to be to dissociate speech and gesture to some extent, and to give the latter its full breadth and meaning through the "double." The resulting slowness recalled the rhythm of Nō drama.

The effect, as Darius Milhaud remarks, was a little like that of a musical accompaniment, also dissociated from the text as Claudel wished, unfolding "a sort of tapestry of sound in the background." It was also very near to that produced by the use of film in *Le Livre de Christophe Colomb*, first introduced in the performances in Germany in 1930. The object was to create a background by throwing onto the screen either the images in the character's mind, or landscapes recalling his travels, or even the scene taking place on the stage at that moment —but played in a different way or seen from a different angle—or perhaps an enlarged detail from that scene. In this way the action was duplicated and so gained in intensity. Other simpler ways of using film are possible and Claudel thought of these also, always making the very most of his idea. The stage directions in the first version of *L'Histoire de Tobie et de Sara*, for example, suggest that a moving set should be used, a screen instead of a backcloth. It was more tempting to use film for certain scenes that were difficult to do, or in which the physical presence of the actor might have given a wrong impression. It was considered at a very early stage for the transformations of Proteus, and Claudel tried in vain to have it accepted as a solution for the scene of the Double Shadow. The cinema, he felt, could be one of the elements of this "total art," providing the text with a firm support which the actors could not give and, as he said of *L'Histoire de Tobie et de Sara*, bringing perspective to the play and giving it the crowning touch.

Another very similar notion is that of the inner stage, or *Guignol*, as Claudel called it. He often comes back to it, and although his explanations are not very detailed, we imagine that it was especially intended for plays with a chorus that would be placed on the normal stage and would act as an intermediary between the actors and the audience. This would signify its proper place in the production. But Claudel was probably also aiming at effects like those which could be achieved by the cinema—two actions going on simultaneously, or one action taking place on two levels, which would change from one scene to another. In his first notes on production he deplored the fact that the size of the stage could not be changed, but the double stage made all sorts of variations possible.

It will have been noticed that every one of these inventions appears to tend toward the intensification of theatrical illusion—the duplication of actor and action, a commentary in music or film, an inner stage isolating the actors and moving them away from the audience. A good example is *Le Soulier de satin* where the appearances of the Announcer or the Irrépressible have the same effect as the use of an inner stage. We remember how Claudel admired the Bunraku puppets (even before he knew them, he had written a puppet play, *L'Ours et la lune*, and tried to get it performed). What he says about this form of Japanese theatre helps us to understand his reasoning: the puppet frees the theatre from realism. (In the same way, Claudel was attracted to the radio because it liberated the text "from the coarseness of gesture and bodily movements.") In Bunraku everything happens in a sort of dream. Nothing intervenes between the play and the audience or between the poet and the audience: "It is not an actor speaking, but speech acting."

Two quite different ideas should be distinguished and followed up separately. First of all, there is Claudel's continual desire to subordinate setting, movement, and all the other components of the theatre to the text, or rather to use them to give the play its full scope and value. So when Claudel speaks of the "liberation" of the text in Bunraku, he is not expressing contempt for the actor; perhaps he is merely regretting that the actor is not usually as adaptable and obedient as the puppet.

The image of the dream is certainly more interesting. It seems to have had some importance for Claudel. The starting point of *Le Livre de Christophe Colomb* was borrowed from Bunraku in which the text is read by a narrator. It is a small detail but a significant one. The play does indeed take the form of a dream or rather an action in the mind and memory of Christopher Columbus. The same applies to *Jeanne d'Arc au bûcher*. The ballets, *L'Homme et son désir* and *La Femme et son ombre*, and the mime play, *Le Peuple des hommes cassés*, are also shown as dreams, but "constructed" dreams, having only the appearance of dreams, not their movements. Claudel's inspiration does not seem to be based on dreams. However, late in life he defined drama as a "guided dream." He also emphasized very frequently—when writing about certain of his works—the "nonexistence" of his characters, which were simply divergent and contradictory aspects of himself. Later he expressed a very similar idea with a different justification—that his characters were simply the actors in a "parable." As he says of *Le Soulier de satin*, "The play is only the means by which the event, the moment of change, the essential and central conflict on which all human life is based, is isolated, outlined, completed, illustrated, and given its place in the domain of both the general and the particular." This theme of the parable reappears when he writes of *Partage de midi* and *L'Histoire de Tobie et de Sara*. It has been considered, perhaps rightly, a belated defense of some of his plays. But for Claudel it was a return to one of his earliest ideas on the theatre, expressed, as we shall see, in a letter to Pottecher in 1899. Playing with words as he loved to do, he took the statement that the poet speaks *for* the people, and commented that this did not mean *for the benefit* of the people, but *on behalf of* the people. He explained: "He *purges* the masses of the unformed aspirations that struggle confusedly within them. This seems to have been the idea of the classical theatre with its single protagonist emerging from the anonymity of the chorus and going back to it again." He admitted that, for his part, he preferred this conception to that of the modern theatre which aims either to entertain or to instruct. His theatre is a theatre of parables, because its themes are, he believes, general ones, of direct concern to the spectator.

This idea, of a solitary actor facing the chorus, links together certain themes which appear several times in these texts. Speaking of *Jeanne d'Arc au bûcher*, Claudel remarks that he has at last fulfilled his long-standing wish to write a dithyramb, with one character alone before a crowd. He had already framed the story of Christopher Columbus in this way—one man alone, explaining himself. We naturally think of a scene in *Le Soulier de satin*, that of Rodrigo's big speech: "Officers, comrades-in-arms, men assembled here, breathing vaguely around me in the darkness." The situation is exactly the same. Surely it must have obsessed Claudel, for it is the situation of the poet. "One solitary figure, the only one with a face of his own, speaking amid a semicircle of voices, which, simply by being there, lure and compel him to speech. Every poet has known this auditory horizon, this confused murmur of jumbled phrases, echoing and reechoing until at last they give birth to words." Is it an inner voice he means, or is it already a dialogue between the poet and the audience?

More than any other kind of poet, the dramatist speaks *for* the people: "Drama gives concrete form to one of those unformulated, more or less meaningful controversies among which our daily life moves continually. It completes it, authenticates it, raises it to the status of an example." In this product of his later years, he speaks of the birth of drama: "Gradually everything becomes organized." It was an old dream of his to make this transition from daily life to drama or parable obvious in the acting, a dream which gave rise to his ideal of the "theatre in the process of birth." He tried to put this into practice in *Le Ravissement de Scapin* and he would especially have liked to do it in the third version of *Tête d'or*. This version would have shown prisoners of war in a German camp rehearsing the play, bringing it to life and gradually living it themselves, up to the point—quite easy to imagine—when it is impossible to tell where the play stops and life begins. The play would then appear as the transition between daily life and its deeper meaning. Less systematically, he brought this movement into *Le Soulier de satin* and *Le Livre de Christophe Colomb*. The example of *Tête d'or* shows that this is neither a trick nor a superficial demonstration of theatrical illusion. Apart from the meaning it gives to the play, we can see in it an appeal to the audience to become, not merely spectators, but accomplices and even participants. The drama is, after all, their own. Much earlier than this Claudel imagined a performance of the *Eumenides* in which the audience, seated on the steps of the Roman theatre at Orange, represented the people of Athens summoned to judge Orestes.

In these circumstances it becomes easier to understand his continued interest in the problem of the chorus. This is the real public, watching and participating in the action, commenting on it and uttering responses like the responses of the congregation in church. This liturgical simile is Claudel's own, and arose quite naturally when he spoke of the chorus without any idea of separation but, on the contrary, of active participation. The chorus takes over the audience's role of participant. When he thought it feasible, Claudel was glad to give it such a part. It was not often possible but, as we have seen, its place could be taken by music, and even apart from the Announcer and the Irrépressible, we find other devices introduced for the same purpose.

This need for the audience to share in the action of the play is essential to Claudel. Perhaps it is even the basis of all his ideas and all his work on the art of the theatre. He knew in his innermost being that this perfect communion could not be achieved by a realistic imitation of life without robbing the play of all meaning; it must come from a transfiguring of everyday things through poetry, through movement—as

Nijinsky taught him—and through the sets, as he learned from Nō drama. Perhaps we should look even further for the origin of this feeling and of certain other ideas. The type of drama of which Claudel dreamed is implicitly—and even, on some points, very clearly—defined in a prose poem from *Connaissance de l'est*, written in 1897. We shall have to return to this after reading and analyzing the technical passages, because it shows the surprising stability of Claudel's opinions despite all their apparent mutability. Everything is there: the notion of the dream, also expressed by Lechy—"Thought slumbers, and lives only in the sights which we show it"; the part played by music, with the orchestra "replying for the audience"; the actor who ceases to be anything more than "a gesture and a voice"; and above all the intense participation by the audience—"The play is tossed by the living breath of the people."

This close bond is achieved through unreality, or at least through an art that is unashamedly stylized. The exposure of stage illusion, far from destroying this movement, strengthens it. Audiences do not come to the theatre in search of the realities of life, unless these realities have become parables and have been given a deeper meaning by virtue of poetry. The words regain their importance, for the bond to be established is between the public and the poet, not the actor, who is merely an intermediary and sometimes an embarrassing one. For that reason Claudel tries to force on the actor his own aesthetic conception of what the movements and diction should be like. He only wished that the actor could be, as in China, "nothing but a gesture and a voice." Particularly in *Le Soulier de satin*, he goes over the actor's head to enter into a sort of conspiracy with the audience: "All these various beings have given up their own preoccupations and personalities. They have handed over the right of speech to the poet. All that remains is attentive silence, and a strange state of collective, almost hypnotic, receptivity." The poet is speaking *for* them.

Jacques Petit and Jean-Pierre Kempf.

Our thanks are due to Mme. Renée Nantet and M. Pierre Claudel, and most particularly to Charles Galperine, whose help and advice have been invaluable.

Part I

The Years of Apprenticeship

The Poet Without a Theatre

In the very first versions of *Tête d'or* and *La Ville* we see that Claudel was already thinking systematically about the theatre, but he obviously did not give serious thought to the production of his plays until *L'Échange*. Then, however, the idea of public performance began to take shape. Claudel himself implies this when he remarks that his play conforms to the "unities," and states it more explicitly in a letter to Pottecher dated 19 July 1894:

I have finished my new play, *L'Échange*. It is rather short—only 80 fairly small pages—has only four characters, and conforms to the three unities in all three acts. I've had a vague idea from time to time of having it produced, but you know how easily I get these ideas and then drop them. At the moment I'm copying out *Tête d'or* (second version—I finished that two weeks ago).

I hope you will derive some real pleasure from your visit to Bayreuth. I've always wanted to go there, though quite honestly I don't know whether I should learn much from it. Is it really possible to create a "theatre of ideas"? And even if you can get the public to watch that sort of play, it is going to have any lasting effect on them? It's an idea I've had for a long time, and whenever I think of it I come up against very serious difficulties. I think it would clear my mind if I tried it, and one of these days I will, even if I have to do it under indifferent conditions.[1]

Some time later Pottecher founded the *Théâtre du peuple*. On 26 February 1897, Claudel had this to say about the experiment:

Congratulations on your enterprise. It is a noble effort which can only lend strength to your activity as a poet. But to me any theatrical production is like a pen stabbing at blank paper—merely the outward expression of the idea. It may give a more stirring call to action, but direct moral influence is beyond it. The transformation of a soul involves forces as deep-rooted as its creation. You need personal contact, a sort of communion that must be both intimate and far-ranging, and a dramatic performance cannot provide this—even less than a book, over which eyes and mind can linger. The great delight—the only delight—of the theatre is that it can give concrete form to the poet's dream.[2]

> And later still, after reading Le Théâtre du Peuple (1899), he wrote to the same correspondent:

I have, of course, read your book on Art and the People with great interest. I can think of no more absorbing question for a writer, particularly a dramatist. It seems to me that however much one ponders on the subject, there are only two conclusions to be reached:

The writer may speak to the people, directly, either to entertain or to instruct. This is the modern conception of the theatre. Whether the audience consists of fashionable society, as at the Théâtre-Français, or children, as at the circus, or the moujiks who went to see Tolstoy's plays, or the peasants of Bussang, the poet's efforts still have an object which is rather more than that of listening to his own voice.

Or, the writer may speak *on behalf of* the people, who, as soon as the actor opens his mouth, show by their silence that they all agree to this common delegation of authority. On the stage or elsewhere, he relieves and *purges* the masses of the unformed aspirations that struggle confusedly within them. This seems to have been the idea of the classical theatre, with its single protagonist emerging from the anonymity of the chorus, and going back to it again.[3]

> Contempt and curiosity! A little contempt—perhaps rather affected, since he called L'Échange "my new puppet show." A great deal of curiosity; there is no other way to explain the character of Lechy Elbernon in L'Échange:

LECHY ELBERNON: The theatre. Don't you know what it is?
MARTHE: No.
LECHY ELBERNON: You have the stage, and you have the audience.
And in the evening, when everything's closed, they come, and they sit in rows, one behind the other, and they look.

MARTHE: What do they look at, if everything is shut?

LECHY ELBERNON: They look at the curtain. And at what is behind it when it rises.

And something happens on the stage, just as though it were real.

MARTHE: But it isn't real! It's like the dreams you have when you're asleep.

LECHY ELBERNON: That's why they come to the theatre at night.

THOMAS POLLOCK NAGEOIRE: She's right. And even if it were real, what does it matter?

LECHY ELBERNON: I look at them, and they are all just living, clothed flesh.

And they cluster on the walls like flies, right up to the ceiling.

And I see those hundreds of white faces.

Man lives his life in boredom, and ignorance clings to him from his birth.

And because he does not know how anything begins or ends, he goes to the theatre.

And he sits with his hands on his knees, and looks at himself.

And he laughs and cries, and cannot bear to leave.

And I look at them, and I know that there among them is the cashier who knows that tomorrow

The books will be checked, and the adulterous mother whose child has fallen ill,

And the man who has just stolen for the first time, and the man who has done nothing all day,

And they look and listen as though asleep.

MARTHE: The eye is made to see, and the ear

To hear the truth.

LECHY ELBERNON: What is truth? Is it not like an onion, with seventeen skins?

Who can see things as they are? The eye sees, the ear hears

But only the mind knows. And that is why man

Longs to take out what he carries in his mind,

To see it with his eyes and know it with his ears.

And so I show myself on the stage.

MARTHE: Are you not ashamed?

LECHY ELBERNON: I am not ashamed! I show myself, and I am all things to all people.

They listen to me and they think what I say; they look at me and I enter their soul like an empty house.

I play the women:
The young girl, and the virtuous wife with a blue vein on her
temple, and the deceived courtesan.
And when I scream, I hear the whole audience moaning.[4]

> A glance through the second version of *Tête d'or* is enough to
> show this preoccupation. The poet can already see it on the stage.
> Sometimes words give place to gestures; the Princess' long speech
> when she enters in the second act is replaced by these stage direc-
> tions:

She throws back her veil and gazes before her.
Tête d'or is standing, crowned, sword in hand, his feet on the King's
flowing robe. On his right are the King's Brother and the Magistrates of
the Republic, and on his left the Representatives of the People. The
company falls back in two lines, leaving a clear way to the door.
The Princess slowly opens her arms, and, kneeling, kisses the ground
and remains in that position.

Two women take her arms and raise her, and she stands before
Tête d'or, her head bowed on her chest.
Silence.[5]

> Other stage directions show a craving for the spectacular—for
> example, when, in the third act, the body of Tête d'or appears:

The rope is let down, after a wide platform has been secured to it
by means of chains.
The soldiers hoist it by means of a pulley. And soon the group of
Captains comes out of the abyss on to the platform, on which lies the
body of Tête d'or; they are so eager that some have their legs dangling
in space, and others are clinging to the chains.
The group rises to the height of the sun which covers it, then the
pulley runs back and the platform slowly descends to the ground, and
they alight.[6]

> Such stage directions give us some insight into Claudel's conflict-
> ing tastes, for a simplified kind of theatre where movement is every-
> thing, and for elaborate scenes making use of every possible
> technical resource.
> The Chinese theatre, which he had already discovered in New
> York—he mentions it in a letter to Schwob—and often visited in
> Shanghai, gratified the first of these tastes. He devoted to it one of
> the prose poems in *Connaissance de l'est*:

Theatre

The palace of the Corporation of Canton has the shrine of its golden god, its inner room, where great thrones, placed solemnly in the middle, stand empty, commanding rather than inviting one to rest. As European clubs have their libraries, here we have the theatre, established with pomp and circumstance on the other side of the courtyard which fronts the whole building. It is a stone terrace set back between two buildings; the stage is a high upright block, marked only by the difference in level as it towers above the heads of the crowd like a great flat step. A square roof shades it like a canopy over an altar, and a second portico in front of it, framing it with its four pillars, lends it remoteness and solemnity. Comedy grows there, legends become their own storytellers, and the vision of what has been is revealed in a rumble of thunder.

The curtain, which is like the veil dividing sleep from wakefulness, does not exist here. But as though each character, snatching away his own shred, had become caught up in the impassable silken barrier whose colors and illusive gleam are like the trappings of night, their robes reveal nothing but the movement beneath. Under the fine feathers of his part, his head dressed with gold, his face hidden beneath paint and mask, each is but a gesture and a voice. The emperor mourns for his kingdom, the unjustly accused princess flees among monsters and savages, armies march past, battles are waged, years and miles are wiped out with a wave of the hand, old men listen to arguments, the gods descend, and a demon rises from a cauldron. But as though performing a song or a complicated dance, not one of these characters ever wavers from the rhythm or from the pattern that measures distances and governs movements. They would as soon fling off their enveloping robes. Behind them the orchestra pours forth its stirring tumult all through the play, as though, like bees swarming at the beating of an iron pot, the phantoms on the stage would disappear with silence; or perhaps it is the music that holds everything together, acting as prompter, replying on the audience's behalf. It slows the movement or hurries it on, gives a sharper accent to the actor's speech, or, rising behind him, blows the sound back into his own ears. There are guitars, pieces of wood which are beaten like drums or rattled like castanets, a sort of one-stringed violin which, like a fountain in an empty courtyard, follows the development of an elegy with its plaintive thread of music, and finally, in the heroic episodes, the trumpet. This is a kind of bugle with a brass bell, and its note, rich in harmonics, has an incredible brilliance and a terrifying penetration. It is like the bray of an ass, a cry in the desert, a fanfare to the sun, the clamor vented from an elephant's trunk. But the chief place belongs to the gongs and cymbals whose discordant noise excites and prepares the nerves and dulls the mind so that, in a sort of slumber, it sees only the sights offered to it. And in wicker cages hung at the side of the stage, two dovelike birds (I am told they are called *Pelitze* and come from Tientsin), innocently rivaling the clamor surrounding them, spin a celestial thread of sound.

The hall under the second portico, and the whole courtyard, are completely filled with a mass of living heads from which rise the pillars and the two sandstone lions with jaws like toads, wearing clusters of children on their heads. It is a pavement of round yellow faces, pressed so close that no bodies or limbs can be seen; they form a solid mass, their hearts beating one against the other. The whole sways together; sometimes, stretching out a row of arms, it is thrown against the stone wall of the stage, and sometimes it falls back and swerves out to the side. In the upper galleries, rich men and mandarins smoke their pipes and drink tea from cups with brass saucers, looking down like gods on the play and the audience. Just as the actors are hidden in their robes, so the play stirs beneath the living tissue of the crowd, as though it were going on in its very heart.[7]

> In February 1911—none of his plays had yet been performed, but he had had many requests—he noted in his journal his demands with regard to the theatre:

Ideas on production:

1. Avoid perches, borders, etc., everything that gives the stage its lack of solidity, its look of cardboard and canvas. I claim the right to a third dimension. For example, a tree must be represented by a real cylindrical object and not a painted optical illusion. A flat surface can give the effect of a third dimension only if you are facing it, seeing it from one angle only. That is the case with pictures, not with the theatre, where the audience sees only the backcloth from directly in front, and everything else obliquely. A material must be found which is not stiff like canvas glued to laths, but light and malleable, yet keeping the shape into which you mold it. If there is an optical illusion it must be achieved not by painting but by sculpture.

2. The colors are completely wrong, never accurate. This is because

the scene is composed of planes, not volumes. Shadows are not possible.

3. We should do away with footlights or, in any case, use a lighting which casts shadows all from the same side. The difficulty is that in the theatre the characters are almost always silhouetted against the back-cloth which is supposed to represent the illuminated part.

4. The set should not always be the same size whether the scene is an intimate one or a vast concourse. Every scene has its own most suitable volume of space around it. It ought to be possible to decrease the size of the stage when required. This would also save the actors from having to use the whole stage in movements which are both unnatural and tiring.

5. No completely new clothes.

6. The stage should be covered so that the boards cannot be seen.[8]

First Contacts with the Theatre

It was not until the end of 1912 that Claudel had any real contact with the theatre or had anything to do with a production. When Lugné-Poe produced *L'Annonce faite à Marie*, the poet insisted on having his say. These "quite new problems" fascinated him, even though he complained a little about the excitement and the waste of time.

On 8 December 1912, he wrote to Gide "Far from being repelled by these problems of stage management, I find them extremely interesting. It is really fascinating to work on a piece of business, a movement or a grouping, and to see it all taking shape." As early as 15 November, he wrote to Jammes, "The work being done on gesture and speech is most interesting to me."

He did not, however, give the designer absolute freedom, although on this point his ideas are less clear and his demands somewhat contradictory. On 21 September he wrote to Lugné-Poe: "I'm rather concerned about the sets. We must avoid pasteboard and optical illusions, and yet the play should not appear to be taking place in a dream."

THE SETS

We have nothing by Claudel himself on this subject, but it is interesting to note the reflection of the poet's ideas in the article which Jean Variot wrote for the programme of the Théâtre de L'Oeuvre.

The sets for *L'Annonce faite à Marie*

The theatre where we play has a small stage (which does not altogether displease us, as we have noticed that actors often tend to *appear lost on a big stage),* and we are very short of money. In view of these things we had to decide between various possible types of sets. We began by considering two possibilities:*

1. *A fixed background such as Julius Klein used for* Jedermann: *the actors play in front of it, and projectors are used for varied effects.*

2. *The stage is divided into two sections as in the Kunstlertheater. The first section, or proscenium, has a curtain on each side; the second has a backcloth which changes for the different scenes.*

We chose the second method. Paul Claudel pointed out to us that in his play the characters are continually making very clear references to the things around them. When Violaine says "I have opened the door," Claudel wants us to see a door, not merely a curtain. As the author's wish must take precedence over the producer's, our decision is easily understood.

Paul Claudel's stage directions are extremely detailed. Characters and scenes are minutely described, and for that reason L'Annonce faite à Marie *was very difficult to fit in to a simplified set. To give some idea of this difficulty I can say that the variety of scenes is almost as complicated as in the old Spanish theatre, which, as you know, is usually one long ramble through palaces, forests, gardens, and so on.*

In an endeavor to give certain scenes the appearance of a holy picture, we have put a sort of decorated frame round the whole set, to produce the necessary stylized effect.

The two curtains on the right and left of the proscenium are the equivalent of the architectural motifs in the same positions at the Kunstlertheater which we mentioned earlier. They have the advantage of taking up more or less room according to the different scenes.

PROLOGUE: The barn at Combernon———*The backcloth has a door, decorated, according to Claudel's directions, with the images of St. Peter and St. Paul. All is dark. A torch casts a feeble light. Pale beams of daylight come through when Violaine opens the door, and the figure of Pierre de Craon stands out against the lighted wall. The great simplicity of the set should, we feel, contribute to the majesty of this prologue.*

ACT I: The kitchen at Combernon———*The fireplace stands against the backcloth. The proscenium curtains are drawn back slightly toward*

---

* It is also interesting to note the proportions of the figures in the paintings of the Italian primitives, particularly those of the school of Siena. The figures are large in the picture and a mere handful represents a crowd. On the basis of this fact, we prefer a small stage to a big one.—J. V.

the front of the stage, giving the illusion that daylight is entering the room through doors and windows at the side. The lighting is arranged in such a way that it is impossible to recognize the set used for the prologue, which is, however, unchanged.

ACT II: Monsanvierge and the Adoue Fountain—*The proscenium curtains are drawn completely to the front of the stage. The fountain is placed in the very center of the proscenium, so that the two characters, Violaine and Jacques Hury, form a group which at once compels attention. Their dialogue is the starting point of the drama. The backcloth shows the towers of Monsanvierge, almost like a piece of embroidery, treated in such a way that the picturesqueness of the scenery is dissociated from the action. It is, as it were, a frame for Violaine and Jacques Hury. The lighting is brilliant.*

ACT III: The trees of Chevoche——*The proscenium curtains are as before. It is the backcloth which changes, showing a row of tree trunks with lopped branches. This scene is played very rapidly. The light is dim.*

For the famous scene between Violaine and Mara, the two women are surrounded by utter darkness. As the singing rises, sporadic gleams of light appear, and at the moment of the final miracle the darkness gives place to a starry sky.

To tell the truth we are only half satisfied with this oversimple solution, but we could do no more with our present resources.

ACT IV: Scene I——*The room as for the first act.*

ACT V: The tree at the bottom of the garden——*This set was made according to our model, a drawing of which appears on the front of this copy.*

Here we have tried to get a general effect like the religious paintings of the Primitives. A scene with the austere grandeur of this one called for special attention. The three characters, Anne Vercors, Pierre de Craon, and Jacques Hury, are standing under the tree which is laden with fruit. We wanted these three figures to appear in a setting of symmetrical lines. We brought the backcloth farther downstage so that the characters could be placed very near to it. Claudel says in his stage directions that the trees and the leaves give the effect of a tapestry. We could not possibly ignore this expressed wish, and we carried out the work as though the aim were not to paint a stage backcloth, but to make a harmonious pattern of shapes and colors with Claudel's three figures, who stand looking upward as in a painting of the school of Siena.

We were lucky enough to have an artist of Rottenstein's strength, and though our setting may not be perfect, it has at least the advantage of not getting in the way of the play.

Jean Variot[9]

DICTION AND GESTURE

Before stating his intentions and requirements in the programme, Claudel confided them to Marie Kalff, writing in March 1912:

If I were to take the liberty to advise you on the interpretation of my plays, I would draw your attention to the following principles:

1. The *music* of the verse is more important than its *sense*.

2. Don't try to bring out every single nuance and charge every word with meaning as they do at the Théâtre-Français. Simply get yourself into such a frame of mind that the words are the obvious natural expression of the character's thought.

3. *Avoid unnecessary movements and facial expressions.* There is nothing more beautiful and more tragic than complete immobility. Always prefer *attitudes* to *gestures.*

Respect the lines of my verse. They should guide you in both the breathing and the emotional rhythm.[10]

And later, on 19 November, after Marie Kalff had fallen ill and had had to give up the part of Violaine and go to Davos for a cure, he wrote:

I have had absolutely no news about my play. I suppose they are too busy with the routine work of learning lines. I think I shall get the intonation fairly near to what I want, especially with Mme. Iribe. I have studied the subject, and have already learned a lot—for example, that the consonant, not the vowel, should take the stress, and that it is more effective to let the accent fall on the very last syllable. For example, it is much more emphatic to say, instead of

. . . ce petit être qui *criiie*
. . . ce petit être qui *crrrie*

and instead of

. . . l'obscurcissement comme d'un *ombrage* très obscur
. . . l'obscurcissement comme d'un ombrage très *obscur*

I am still rather worried about gesture, because I no longer have anything to do with that, and Lara seemed stupefied when I told her that you can't rely for gestures on the inspiration of the moment, but must study them as carefully as you do intonations.

The problem is to achieve something beautiful, moving, and easy at the same time. I don't know whether I shall have enough rehearsals for that. . . .

I shall go to Paris on about the 3rd. Good old Poe has a voice like thunder, and the "Pierre de Craon" they've given me has a voice like a chorister's. It's not quite what we need for the opera-style finale.[11]

Finally, the programme contained the following notes:

My Ideas on the General Method to be Used for My Plays

1. The actor is an artist, not a critic. His job is not to explain a text, but to bring a character to life. He must be completely imbued with the thought and feeling of the person he is playing, so that the words he utters on stage must appear to be simply his natural mode of expression. The aim is not to scatter subtle shadings and delicate points of color equally and indifferently over the whole play, but to bring out in every scene the highlights which dominate all the rest. Often we are moved not so much by what the actor says as by what we feel he is about to say. To understand as an intelligent man and to understand as an artist and creator are two completely different things, and it is only by being absolutely clear about their relative importance that an actor can build up his part.

2. The most important thing for me, after the emotion, is the *music*. A pleasant voice, articulating clearly, forming a perfect concord with other voices in dialogue is a feast for the mind, even independently of the abstract meaning of the words. Poetry, with its subtle feeling for timbre and harmony, its images and its movements that reach one's very soul, gives the fullest possible scope to the human voice. The division into *lines* which I have adopted is based on the rhythm of breathing, and breaks the phrase up into units which are not logical but emotional; it should, I think, make study easier for the actor. When we listen to someone speaking, we hear the voice rise at a variable point about the

middle of the sentence, and fall at the end. These two climaxes and the inflections which come between, form the lines of my verse.

The foregoing remarks are not meant to worry the actor nor to force him into a soul-destroying, mechanical type of delivery. It is enough for him to keep this idea in mind, and be guided by it in his general style of speaking.

Because music, to me, is all-important, I am on my guard against anything too violent, jerky, or abrupt in the delivery. The sort of enchantment which links the characters together must not be broken. It seems to me quite possible to reach the hearts of the audience, to be bitter and poignant, without too much violence. If there must be shrieks, they will be the more effective for being rare.

I simply throw out this idea with the modesty and restraint proper to a man who has had as little to do with the theatre as I have.

3. In movement and gesture, too, anything brusque, violent, artificial, or jerky should be avoided, and there should always be a feeling for grouping and attitude. I have a particular horror of what I call a stage walk: two big steps and one little one, followed by a halt. No grimaces or convulsions. In dramatic moments a gesture which unfolds slowly and tragically is better than any outburst. But here too the actor should beware of mannerisms and affectation, and do as his heart tells him.

The principle of great art is an absolute avoidance of anything unnecessary. And it is quite unnecessary to stride constantly up and down on the pretext of using the whole stage, or to be always getting up, turning round and sitting down again. Nothing irritates me so much as an actor who tries to show in detail in his face every single emotion provoked by his partner's speech. He should be able to remain calm and motionless when necessary, even at the cost of a certain awkwardness for which the audience will, at bottom, be grateful.

Every moment of the drama has its corresponding attitude, and gestures should be merely the taking up and the breaking of this attitude.

These remarks, like all the others, are intended to make the actor think. Only he knows what he can do, and my purpose is not to put obstacles in his path, to strangle him, or to turn him into a sort of puppet.

Acting is not primarily for the benefit of the public. The actor, like all great artists, should be disinterested, concerned not with success, but with the best interpretation of the work of art to which he must give life. And it is perhaps by this very indifference to the public that he is able to reach its heart.[12]

Other productions were soon to come: *L'Échange*, produced by Jacques Copeau, at the Vieux-Colombier, and *L'Otage*, produced by Lugné-Poe. But first Claudel discovered the "ideal theatre" at the Institute of Art at Hellerau.

The Spell of Hellerau

Now that Claudel's letters to Lugné-Poe have been published, and his anonymous articles have been identified, and since the research carried out by René Farabet (*Cahier Claudel 5*), we can see more clearly what importance the poet attached to these few performances in 1913.

A German adaptation of *L'Annonce faite à Marie* was given at the Institute of Art at Hellerau near Dresden. In the course of rehearsals Claudel discovered an "experimental theatre" which filled him with enthusiasm. He tried in vain to win over his friends Copeau and Lugné-Poe; he sent for Darius Milhaud, and also published two unsigned articles, the first in *La Nouvelle Revue Française* for September 1913, and the other in *Comœdia* on 4 October.[13]

On the Theatre of Hellerau

The following passage is taken from a letter which one of our correspondents wrote from Germany:

We go to Hellerau to see two things:

1. Music, alive and visible in the human body.

Between music and the body there is a common element, movement, a common measure, time, and a common expression, rhythm. The aim of M. Jaques-Dalcroze is not to teach his pupils dancing or gymnastics. He teaches them to listen to music, not passively, but participating with their whole being, their whole body. For instance, while their steps follow the melody as it quickens or diminishes its speed, the movement of their arms marks the essential rhythm. The musical phrase animates and is itself animated; it follows, governs, inspires, unfolds, and develops the gestures, attitudes, and steps which come naturally to our bodies, but which in daily life have no chance to find more than timid, random and stilted expression. I have seen girls conduct a choir or an orchestra, not with a baton like the usual black-coated gentleman, but with their whole bodies, every movement following and leading at the same time, listening to every part and sweeping the whole thing forward. When the body has completely submitted itself to music, it is sometimes as though it had been created by it.

Such training probably corresponds to what the ancients meant by *music*, and its educational advantages are many and great. It teaches concentration, proportion, self-possession, the control of our impulses, and harmony with all the other movements around us. The body grows pliant and obeys the soul, which in its turn respects the instrument which has to give it visible life.

There is no need to stress the aesthetic results of this method, particularly from the point of view of the theatre. Choruses are no longer rows of miserable lifeless dummies, but become great sentient beings, utterly filled and animated by the life of the drama and the music. From this point of view, the performances of Gluck's *Orpheus* at Hellerau were incomparable. It was the first time since the days of Greece that true beauty had been seen in the theatre.

2. The theatre.

The theatre of Hellerau, built and equipped by an artist of genius, M. de Salzmann (who is Russian) has no pretensions to be a *salon*, or a temple like Bayreuth, but a workshop, giving the artist the extremely flexible and adaptable resources he needs.

It is a vast rectangle, with no fixed stage. The walls and ceiling are of white material behind which battens of lights are placed at regular intervals. There is no visible source of light. All the lights are controlled at the end of the hall by a switchboard by means of which one person can produce any variations of light and shadow he requires. The ceiling, divided into movable screens, forms a series of projectors, where the light either shines through or is reflected as desired, giving all possible combinations of intensity, movement, and direction. Instead of the harsh glare of the footlights, which flattens the actors against the backcloth and makes the scene look like a color print, washed-out and flashy at the same time, we have a milky, Elysian glow, which gives the much despised third dimension back its glory and turns each figure into a statue, with shadows and highlights modeled as though by the hands of a perfect sculptor. Like music in the Dalcroze system, light brings to life the being it envelops, and works together with him. Instead of the sickly beam or the twopence-colored semblance of light we see on most stages, it is a living creature, fine and free.

The *stage* is not fixed. It is made up of movable sections, each in the form of three steps, which fit into each other to make a rectangular prism. These can be joined to form every possible combination—terraces, walls, columns, staircases, etc. In a few minutes you can have a stage with several levels, like those of the old mystery plays. Shape, height, and depth can be altered at will. Every combination is possible. Painted backcloths, flats, and all the ridiculous paraphernalia of the old-fashioned theatres are done away with, and their place taken by architectural shapes which give the basic lines of the action, along which it is to develop. It is, in fact, a framework prepared for it in advance.

It is easy to see how this kind of conception could make possible, for example, the performance of classical drama, for which modern stages are so ill-adapted.

L'Annonce faite à Marie
By M. Paul Claudel
at the Theatre of Hellerau, Germany

L'Annonce faite à Marie, by M. Paul Claudel which was performed last year in Paris by the company of the Théâtre de L'Oeuvre with resounding success, will be played in Germany, as a *Festspiel*, on October 5, 11, and 19, in a completely new and unusual type of production, before being presented in Berlin by M. Max Reinhardt. The translation, we are told, is by Jacques Hegner.

Our readers have perhaps already heard of the admirable project founded in the little town of Hellerau, near Dresden, by a group of scholars, for the development of the system of "living music and movement" taught by M. Jaques-Dalcroze. Perhaps we shall have the opportunity to return to the subject and tell our readers about the amazing performances of *Orpheus* which took place last July. For the moment we wish simply to describe the practice room and theatre, designed by a Russian artist, Alexander de Salzmann.

It is an elongated rectangle, 42 meters long, 17 meters wide, and 12 meters high. There is no fixed stage; it is built as required from movable units like pieces of a child's construction toy. There are no visible sources of light. The four walls of the room and the ceiling are covered with transparent white material behind which are arranged battens of electric lights. The ceiling is divided into screens which can be raised and serve as projectors. A switchboard allows an operator to play this vast keyboard as he wishes. The light either shines through or is reflected. All possible variations of shade, intensity, and direction are thus obtained. The light follows all the vicissitudes of the action with amazing flexibility and gentleness. It is no crude patchwork of footlights and projectors, but a delightful atmosphere which makes those that move in it living, three-dimensional beings.

For the setting of *L'Annonce,* only these new resources of architecture and light were used. No properties, no painting, no pasteboard. No attempt to be picturesque. The interpretation of the play is everything. The stage only serves to provide a framework for the action by establishing in advance the planes and elevations on which it is to develop.

It is to be noted that the stage is arranged in such a way that every point on it without exception can be seen from every point in the auditorium without exception. There are no hidden corners. Every inch is visible and useful.

As we know, the essential theme of *L'Annonce* is the glorification of the humblest realities and their elevation to the Eternal Kingdom. The hearth becomes the undying flame, the table becomes the altar, and the door becomes Heaven's gate. The producers, using the movable units at their disposal, have therefore designed a stage on various levels. Let us take for example the first act, the father's farewell. This act contains the three scenic *motifs* or "permanent actors" which we have just listed —the hearth, the table, and the door. All three must face the audience; otherwise they will not exist for them. On an ordinary stage, then, we would have to lose two of them. On the stage at Hellerau they are placed one above the other. On the lowest level, in a recess, is the hearth; that is where the first scenes are played. Above is a second level, where the father's farewell and the breaking of bread take place. Higher yet is a third level to which the father ascends to give the supreme blessing to his family. The mother comes down at the same moment to take up her post at the domestic hearth. When the father raises his hands, darkness gradually fills the room, finally engulfing it completely so that we see only the mother, sitting, pensive, in the faint light of the fire.

This arrangement by levels obviously makes it possible for different actions to follow one upon the other in space without any break in continuity and sometimes even to be shown simultaneously. When the curtain rises on the second act, we see the mother on the lowest level, still motionless beside the fire. The short scene with Mara is played there. Then Mara goes up to the second level for the scene with Jacques Hury. She goes out, and at the same time Violaine, all in gold, appears on the third level. She descends to the second, where the big (leprosy)[14] scene is played with Jacques. Then the action continues on the first level where the four characters are grouped for the farewell scene.

M. de Salzmann's lighting makes it possible to vary the psychological and material environment of each scene with wonderful flexibility. It is also used to give earthly actions the crowning effect of the supernatural and the marvelous. On the vast white curtain which forms the background, soft and deep like a real atmosphere, there appears at certain moments, as for example the father's departure, the scene of the miracle and the musical epilogue, a lofty Gothic arch in color, symbolizing the consecration of human prayers and the opening of a better world.

> Claudel took a very active part in the production of his play, and a letter to Lugné-Poe (4 July 1913) leads us to believe that the use of the stage on various levels was his own idea:

My play is to be performed without any set, using simply Salzmann's marvelous lighting and the resources of the sectional stage. My special device consists of using the stage at various levels, which will at last let me apply my theory of "permanent actors," and to let the audience see, in the first act, for example, the fire, the table, and the door, all at once and all in the center of the stage. The farewell scene, which I have tried, takes on an incredible grandeur. I shall develop the staging, too. The Angels will be seen in the third and fourth acts, we shall have the praying women, bell-ringers, etc., and all this very simply arranged.[15]

> For some months Claudel really believed that all his work would be revolutionized by this discovery. He confided to Darius Milhaud that he intended to present *Protée* and the *Oresteia* at Hellerau (6 June 1913), and declared to Lugné-Poe: "The plays I am going to write have no set and can be performed anywhere" (9 October 1913).
> This impression faded, but never entirely disappeared. It gave rise to a project which long obsessed Claudel: to present the *Oresteia* in the Roman theatre at Orange.

The *Oresteia*

The discovery of Hellerau and the meeting with Darius Milhaud inspired Claudel to return to his translation of the *Agamemnon* of Aeschylus, which he had begun much earlier. In 1913 he began to translate the *Choephori*. It took him a long time to finish the *Eumenides*, which may perhaps have been because his plans for staging the plays had fallen through.

He thought at first—as he told Milhaud on 6 June 1913—of having the *Oresteia* produced at Hellerau. Then he had another idea. The three plays could be performed in the perfect setting for them —the Roman theatre at Orange.

As early as 9 July 1914, he was asking Lugné-Poe for information. The questions he puts to him show that he already had plans for the production.

Tell me whether the door is a real door, through which you can enter—also whether the two bastions on each side of the stage are hollow, and what is inside—also whether you can get into the niche above the stage, and if so, how—and the same for the wall and the top of the two bastions. Would it be possible to dig a large pit in the middle of the orchestra?

The reply was scarcely encouraging, but in August 1915 Claudel, who had to go to Aix to see Milhaud, planned "to have another look at the theatre at Orange."

The texts which follow show very clearly what he had in mind.[16] He wanted to use this theatre in the same way as the Hellerau stage, playing on different levels.

They also show that he was concerned with questions of music. The problem he raised—that of fitting the music to the play—was to become more and more important to him.

22 May 1913

Dear Milhaud,

Following our conversation in Paris—

I would be glad if you would read my translation of the *Agamemnon* (*Théâtre*, vol. IV) and tell me what you think of the problem of adding music to the choruses *without detracting from the dramatic effect*. We need something like the note on which the Epistle and Gospel are chanted, which can turn into true song without a break. The question arises especially at the end of the act (dialogue of Clytemnestra and chorus). If you could find the solution, it would be extremely important for the whole of the *Oresteia* and the satyr play I am working on at the moment.

27 May 1913

My dear Milhaud,

Thank you for your very discerning letter, which contains all the objections I have made myself. And yet . . . I *feel* (as an artist feels, quite apart from any reasoning) that the dialogue between Clytemnestra and the choir cannot be simply declaimed without actually becoming music. It was not for nothing that Aeschylus completely altered the rhythm at this point, and made Clytemnestra speak in lyrical verse. At this moment Clytemnestra is filled with a savage, almost devilish joy. She is possessed by a spirit that is almost cannibalistic (in the Greek manner, without ever going beyond the bounds of moderation). Her words must not *sing*, but *dance*. The rhythm must be hammered out with a brutality which ordinary declamation could never achieve. We need a kind of "music" reduced purely to its rhythmic element, for example the beating of drums and other percussion instruments or staccato blasts on the trombone.* Oh, it's so difficult to explain! And yet I *feel* that at this moment speech alone is not enough, although, like you, I find it quite enough for the other parts of the *Agamemnon*. I would like you to read the *Oresteia* all through (in Leconte de Lisle's translation for example, bad though it may be), particularly the *Eumenides* which I imagine ending with a full-throated chorus in the style of Handel.

The edition of the *Choephori* brought out by *La Nouvelle Revue Française* in 1920 contains the following suggestions for production.

---

* This is the part played in the Arab festivals by the public, who, with shouts, drumbeats, and handclapping, support and accompany the dance of the Possessed. This ending of *Agamemnon* is really diabolical.—P. C.

I would prefer a stage made up of movable units, like that at Hellerau in Saxony. But the arrangement shown below is so simple that it could be carried out in any theatre.

A—A curtain of heavy black material falling in ample folds. The women of the chorus enter through slits in it.

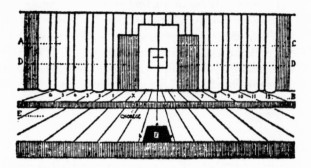

B—A sort of narrow second stage in front of the door, separated from the first one by a step.

C—The Great Door, which remains shut until Orestes appears in its opening, standing over the bodies of Clytemnestra and Aegisthus.

D and D¹—Two smaller doors, long and narrow, on each side of the Great Door. The people of the house come and go through these.

E—The main stage.

F—A rectangular pit in the front of the main stage, representing Agamemnon's tomb. At the moment of the Incantation a wisp of blue smoke, like that from a burning joss stick, rises from it.

The Chorus

This is the main difficulty in performing classical drama exactly as it was written. First of all, we can rule out, without further discussion, all we learned at school about files of men or women weaving one behind the other, as strophe or antistrophe demands, around some sort of altar called a *thymele*, chanting lyric poetry in unison.

For me, the Chorus is the anonymous crowd surrounding the principal actor of the play. They have to provide a reply and an echo to each explosion of his personality, each passionate outcry; he leans on them and appeals to them as official witnesses and spokesmen for the public, in whatever disguise is appropriate to the story.

According to this conception, the part of the chorus in classical drama is very like that of the choir in the liturgy as it is still sung in the old

Roman churches. The dialogue took place between the officiating priest and a group whose task it was to represent the faithful. The old Introit for the First Sunday in Advent is an example.

In *Agamemnon* I would put the Old Men of the chorus quite frankly in the same position as the precentors in our churches, and I would dress them in the same heavy robes, with cope and staff, each installed at his lectern, reading his part, facing the terrible Door through which one actor after another comes out of the night. Eleven of the chorus would be Old Men, and the twelfth would be a child who sometimes, while the others were singing, would amuse himself by playing knucklebones.

In the *Choephori* it was important to avoid the only too obvious opportunity for processions in the academic style with noble poses, attitudes of completely insincere attention, and all the other well-known trappings.

The first alternative I thought of, a procession close on the heels of the primitives (as Raoul says) with carts laden with brilliant-colored fruit and a collection of barbaric ironmongery, had the disadvantage of being nothing more than picturesque, and counterfeit at that.

But as the members of the chorus are mainly expected to speak and sing we could not ask them for mass gymnastic displays and statuesque groups, which are disgusting anyway.

They will, therefore, be dressed simply in white voluminous robes with sculptured folds, and a flowing black cloak with a hood which can hide the face and allow them, at the end, to blend with the curtain and with the Furies who stand out against this background of darkness.

They will hold in their hands a paper on which their part is written, and they will be asked to raise their eyes from it as little as possible.

The costumes of the principal actors must not try to be picturesque or archeologically correct. All we need are those folds, which simplify the lines of the body and lend breadth to the movements.

In the edition of the *Eumenides* published in the same year, Claudel says in a note: "I should have liked to make suggestions for the production of the *Eumenides* as I did for the *Choephori*, but my ideas on the subject, either for the theatre at Orange or that at Hellerau, are not yet properly worked out." A year later, on 9 August 1921, he made some notes on production in a letter to Darius Milhaud:

Dear Friend,

I was very pleasantly surprised to find that you are still interested in the *Eumenides*. I thought you had abandoned the idea. Have you kept the final chorus in the second act? Literally speaking, I like both its rhythm and its broken patterns. Speaking of broken patterns, make any cuts you like in the 3rd act. In my opinion, the words are not important at all. The audience's interest must be aroused without their understanding a single word, simply by the movement and pattern of the phrases, which should not be musically colored but in speech rhythm. I can make my line of thought clearer by giving you a brief plan for the production.

1. Orestes, small and alone, dominated and crushed by the crowd.

2. Athena, ceremonially carried in at the beginning of the act on a sort of litter or palanquin.

3. A sort of hollow room with tiers of seats filled by the crowd.

4 and 4a. Two diagonal paths, crossing and recrossing the whole of this stage from top to bottom.

5. Inner stage or "Guignol" on which Apollo is on one side and the Furies on the other.

At the end two processions are formed, one leading the Furies downward and the other leading Athena upward. The movement can begin during the discussion with Athena, by girls approaching the Furies, pushing them by the shoulders, taking them by the hand, etc.

Musically, I think the play is made for you, because of all its wildly dissimilar and contrasted elements which you have the art to fuse together and mold into something harmonious.

There are three elements:

1. The crowd, filling with constant movement the sort of bowl made for it, accompanying the whole play with its uproar. (I think we could do something wonderful with the vote scene.)

2. The Olympian element which gradually reveals itself and ends by submerging everything in a great flood.

3. The shrill pathetic chatter of the human race, spoken, but accompanied rhythmically. The phrasing and movement must not be solemn and ponderous but violent and rapid. (Orestes is a Levantine, a glib, wily Syrian like those you knew in Brazil.) From this point of view the lines of my verse might lead you astray. It must all be poured forth almost in one breath.

16.8 I have just got back from the Grande Chartreuse, and I see now that all this is mere verbiage. You know better than I what you have to do.

> Finally he speaks of these plans in the preface he wrote for the *Oresteia* on 28 August 1942. He recalls the performances of the *Choephori* in Brussels, and concludes:

As for the *Eumenides*, I think we could still do something really moving with it. It is a typical example of those civic, social, or religious dramas which would be worth the attention of our younger poets. I have always dreamed of a setting like that of Orange. The people on the stone seats would represent the people of Athens and would be themselves a part of the whole magnificent show. The question—still one of pressing interest—would be argued before it. And what an ending—the procession of the Furies, going down, in the glow of smoking torches, beneath the huge paving stone lifted in the center of the orchestra, to heap up beneath the earth the terrible storehouse of Justice.

L'Échange and L'Otage

In 1914 two works by Paul Claudel were performed in Paris: Jacques Copeau put on *L'Échange*, and Lugné-Poe *L'Otage*. Claudel apparently had little to do with the production of this second play. He probably discussed it with his producer, but the latter preferred not to let him come to rehearsals too often. "I assure you," Claudel wrote on 24 April 1914, "that I don't want to make this play any more difficult for you, and if I can't help by being there, I'll stay away without bearing you any grudge."

He had rather more to do with *L'Échange*. He gave the actors very similar advice on diction to that which he had given in 1912. He wrote Copeau a few letters to clarify his own view of the play.[17]

6 December 1913

Give me your general ideas on how the play should be done. I haven't read it for years. However, this is what I think. There are two possibilities: it could either be delicate, gray, harmonious, like chamber music, or violently colored, exaggerated, almost a caricature, like a picture by Van Dongen. I think I should prefer the second way. I should like Marthe alone to be a real woman between three sinister puppets with stiff movements and *impassive* faces (we could almost use masks). The color scheme should be dark and intense, the sea indigo blue ending in waves on the backcloth, and a tobacco-brown covering on the floor. I see Louis Laine in a scarlet shirt, Nageoire in a light summer suit with a green tie and belt, Lechy in a crimson blouse and a blue cravat, and covered with diamonds. Nageoire should be fat, pasty and bald, with a fringe of long black hair at the back, looking like a preacher or like the Secretary of State, Bryan. Lechy should have an enormous straw hat, and her hair in a roll over her forehead; her nose should be short and her chin large. All three should have large crooked mouths.

I am giving you these details partly to explain the psychology of the characters. The whole of the drama consists in the contrast of a living woman with three sinister puppets. At the end, Thomas Pollock should wear black with a formidable top hat. In the third act, Lechy should have a great Spanish shawl of white silk. I hope the actress who plays her will have plenty of temperament. . . .

Nageoire must never take his hat off, nor touch it.

8 December 1913

If Marthe is played in a whining listless sort of way, as actresses tend to play Violaine, the play loses its meaning. Marthe is a *practical* woman, and for stage purposes we shall have to be merciless in pruning the part of a great deal of the surplus poetic vegetation which I couldn't help adding to it.

For Lechy I must have a woman with a really fertile imagination—a *rara avis!* I see her in acts I and II in a riding habit with split skirt, boots and crop, and for act III she should wear a red ball dress in extremely bad taste, and a Spanish shawl (Mme. Berthelot has a magnificent one). She falls flat on the ground, face downward on the carpet, one hand turned palm upward. This broken puppet balances the corpse of Laine. Thomas modestly spreads his cape over her. In act III the main character is Thomas's top hat which must be a very large one and never leave his head. This man in a black coat and top hat violently dragging Laine's corpse by the feet should be rather effective. —In act II add to Louis's costume a silk scarf round his neck.

Here is the basic idea of the whole play: Idealism is represented only by Marthe, who is at the same time the only really *practical* woman. The others, who are people of purely material outlook, are in reality the prey of dreams. However hard Marthe may shake Laine, she cannot awaken this half-savage. In the third act, two of the skittles are down. Only Thomas is still on his feet, and Marthe holds out her hands to this sincere, sorrowful man as though to a grotesque black Pope wearing a moronic civilization like a crown. . . .

Thomas and Lechy must speak through their noses.

29 December 1913

I am returning the sketches today with my remarks on the back. On the whole I like them and they fit in very well with what I want. As for the backcloth, all we need is an indigo line to represent the sea which is the unchanging witness of the drama, a character which never leaves the stage.

31 December 1913

The idea of the hammock is excellent, and completely American, so I agree with it absolutely. We can even use it for stage business. For example, at one moment Marthe can go through the motions of rocking it. —Have you thought about Marthe's costume? For my part, I think it should definitely be blue, with a veil wrapped round her face in the first act to give her a vaguely Oriental appearance. —In the first scene I think Marthe should have a piece of sewing in her lap, and if she works at this it will make the long speeches easier. Ask Kalff to bring out the first line which is very important, and contains the essence of the whole play: La journée qu'*on voit clair* et qui *demeure* jusqu'à ce qu'elle soit finie.

While Laine is talking about the spider, she could be threading her needle.

Lechy is a ham actress, and she must be constantly trying to attract attention to herself when it isn't her turn to speak. So she can put in every possible bit of business she can think of, especially in the first act; for example, doing a cakewalk as she goes out, pushing her head between Thomas and Marthe when she comes in again, mimicking Thomas's gestures as he speaks, half lying in the hammock, speaking in an undertone, with gestures, as though learning a part, etc. . . .

To articulate my lines properly take the example I've just given and *pick out the strong beats*. Say the consonants very clearly. It's the consonants, not the vowels, which give speech its strength and clarity.

> Copeau seems to have acceded to Claudel's wishes, and emphasized in his production the symbolism of the play. The actors "chanted" the text as the poet wanted. One more striking characteristic of Claudel's advice is his preoccupation with apparently unimportant details. It was noted by Eve Francis, speaking of the rehearsals of *L'Otage:*

Claudel alone remained calm, taking an interest in insignificant details such as . . . the length of Turelure's side-whiskers, or Coufontaine's gloves. Should the Pope's girdle, he asked, be black or white? We were anxious, upset, hesitant . . . hanging on his words and longing for encouragement on the interpretation of the script, but he was talking about shoe laces (Temps héroïques, p. 225).

> The performances of *L'Otage* gave rise to some controversy. Certain critics questioned the character of Sygne, and, in consequence,

the "catholicism" of the work. Claudel replied in a letter to *Le Temps*, then in another to *Le Figaro*, "Le Théâtre catholique."[18] After explaining Sygne's attitude, he went further into the problem:

When this question is settled there remains another, which troubled me a great deal in the past; I think this is the time to say a few words about it. I mean the old dispute about the possible relationship between the Catholic religion and the theatre.

The attitude generally attributed to the Church on this question is the one which is strongly defended in Bossuet's famous and admirable letter to Father Caffaro. But dare I say that in spite of the impressive authorities which Bossuet quotes in support of his opinion, it strikes me as a clear example of the defensiveness and retrenchment which are typical of Galicanism? The truly Catholic—which means universal— idea is that man, as he leaves the hands of his Creator, is good (Genesis even says very good). Not one of his faculties, and this includes feeling and imagination, is in itself bad. What is bad is the way in which these same faculties were disturbed and disordered as a result of original sin. A heretic is always someone who attacks the integrity of human nature, denying liberty or grace, chastity or marriage, law or authority, con- stantly impoverishing us in some way or another. When Pascal, for example, follows Montaigne in insulting man's reason, and condemning at birth such natural, rightful human feelings as gratitude for benefits received, he speaks as a heretic. The spirit of the Church is not a spirit of defense, but of conquest. Nothing human is alien to it, art no more than anything else, and dramatic art no more than the others. The Church came, according to the motto of the great Pope who rules us, *instaurare omnia in Christo*; not to destroy anything (except evil) but to bring everything to its final point of perfection. I do not deny that the prac- tice, and I might even say the policing, of an art like the theatre which lives partly by depicting human passions is very difficult. The Church has good reasons for her continually mistrustful attitude toward it.

However, if the theatre, with the extraordinary power it wields over human souls by including them, so to speak, in its own action, can, in some way, be useful to the Faith, so can the Faith in return offer in- estimable benefits, some of which I shall enumerate here.

The first is that every modern man lives, through his faith, in an essentially dramatic environment. The least of his acts is subjected to pitiless criticism, and at the end of his days he faces penalties which are both just and terrible. The Christian, as St. Paul said, is "a spectacle unto the world, and to angels, and to men." He is constantly "on stage."

For him, life is not an incoherent series of vague, unfinished movements, but a play, with a precise meaning and its own dénouement.

The second advantage is that the Faith brings to art a "principle of contradiction." It forbids the virtuoso's empty complacency, forces the artist to ponder and struggle, and turns him against all that is obvious and facile, so that expression becomes for him an instrument of torture. I have spoken elsewhere of this point of view, and shall not return to it here.

The third advantage is that the Faith gives a symbolic character to each of our actions, guilty or not. Isolated though they may be, they happen in the sight of a higher reality—the great drama of Creation and Salvation which is their background and upon which they form a kind of commentary, or parable in action.

Finally, the fourth advantage is that the Faith comforts and liberates our nature by showing it the ultimate end of which it is capable. Through it, all our feelings and passions have a meaning, and can enjoy at last the fullness of their truth. The Catholic theory, in fact, is that man is naturally destined for happiness, and none of the efforts he makes toward this natural goal is in itself bad. Evil exists only because our nature has been warped and corrupted by original sin, and we can no longer choose, among the good things offered to us, the only supreme one which gives all the others their meaning. We can translate this thought into aesthetic language by saying "only Good composes," or, in other words, only the Good has the power to establish, not between a few sentiments but all of them, the perfect and final order that alone can satisfy. Rebellion, human love, and the joy of living *compose* badly, for these sentiments are powerless on their own to weld the whole universe together; they clash impossibly. That is why the ending of *Tristan and Isolde* has always seemed to me paltry and almost ridiculous, and despite all the glamor of the music, I resist it as a man might resist a narcotic.

The purely secular art which began with the Renaissance has had its day, and has at last exhausted its resources. I can see its story typified in Wagner's *Ring*, and the supreme holocaust of Valhalla is to me the final catastrophe of the imagination. Wagner had inevitably realized its powerlessness. That is why he later wrote *Parsifal*, which is, as he says himself, the beginning of a new theatrical era.

> A little later, in a lecture called "Introduction to a Few Works" which he gave on 30 May 1919, he once more explained his conception of drama, with reference to *Le Pain dur:*

I wrote this sequence of plays, only two of which have yet been published, because I felt that when a poet wishes to make a complete and isolated whole, capable of being taken in all at once by both the imagination and the intellect, from a complex, involved story which has a beginning and an end, he cannot always do it within the narrow limits of one generation. Parents bequeath to their children, not only certain physical and moral aptitudes, not only a certain attitude to one or other social environment, or the means—such as fortune or rank—to act in a certain way, or to dispose the things around them as they wish, but a task to finish, seeds to sow and a harvest to reap—in short an unfinished part to play in a drama which goes on after some of its actors have left the stage. Like the Tree of Jesse in old stained glass windows, we see a vast complex of persons and deeds arising from one single human couple; the root of the tree is the common consent of this man and this woman on the day of their marriage.

And just as no creature can exist only within the limits of his own lifetime, no human being can pursue his career in isolation. There lies the error of the violent but bankrupt doctrines of Stirner or Nietzsche. No man is alone, no man can accomplish his task without the conscious or unconscious agreement of a host of others, friends or enemies, good or evil, whose presence implies and demands his own. This is, incidentally, the reason for the strange sympathy that an author feels for all the characters in his plays, without exception, even for those who, as in *Le Pain dur*, do not appear to deserve it. An author takes the same pains and the same pleasure in creating a bad character as a good one; a traitor or a brigand is, to his author, simply a component part of a great whole, and as such has his own interest and his own harmony. But evil can never *compose* as good can. Anyone who, like a perfect musician, can keep constantly in mind the symphony for innumerable instruments in which, though continually facing the unexpected, he has to follow or improvise his part, is what is called a righteous man, which is infinitely more than a superman. His actions are *right*, as we feel with all our heart that a musical note or phrase is *right*, that it comes dutifully in the place where it is expected. The final word on morals was said in one of the books of the Old Testament for which I have the greatest admiration, and which summarizes all that is best in sacred and profane wisdom: *Ne impedias musicam!* "Hinder not music." Act in such a way that your actions and your most secret thoughts not only do not impede the harmony of which you are an element, but actually cause and create it around them.

Without this harmony around it, without these stimuli which set the invisible sounding boards within it vibrating, no human personality could ever know its own possibilities. Outward circumstances help us to reveal our true selves, or, as is popularly—and profoundly—said, "come out of ourselves." And what comes out is often, to our great surprise, an almost entirely new and unknown being. In this respect the famous maxim of Socrates "Know thyself" seems to me impracticable. A man who is trying to know himself, and so has to look at himself, can see nothing but powers and faculties yet unformed until some definite act gives them life. . . . The true Christian motto is the opposite of that of Socrates, not "Know thyself" but "Forget thyself." In other words: Turn your attention to something other than yourself, either to God or to those people and things toward whom you have a duty to do. Take care not to miss the call you may hear within the hour, and which may never be repeated. Do not lose yourself in contemplation, or, which would be more ridiculous, in sterile admiration of yourself. For in order to see yourself, you must halt, and place yourself in an artificial attitude —pose, in fact. Do not be stupid enough to say, as lazy people do, that something or other is beyond you, or not in your nature, for how can you tell? The important thing for a man is not what he can do, but what is asked of him. He must look, not at his reflection in a mirror, but at the Cross or the flag! He must listen, not to the dull, frivolous music of dreams and fancies, but to the call which brought him out of the darkness and which has a magnificent name: "vocation."

You will tell me that these are very general considerations for a mere introduction to a programme. Nevertheless, they may go some way toward helping you to understand the work of a dramatist, a man obliged by his profession to ponder on the motivation of several characters brought from every corner of the memory or imagination to carry out one single action. In real life, as we believe, people's characters explain their actions, whereas here the action is decided in advance, and the characters suggested by it. But once the general plot is established and each fictional character given his part in it, the author does not have the arbitrary and absolute authority over them that one would suppose. He is surprised himself by the independence they show, the advice they give him, and sometimes their absolute refusal to do as he asks. He has created a sort of small-scale universe, an artificially simplified society, rather as though he were carrying out a scientific experiment. And though it may be a small-scale universe, once its elements are set going they develop according to a logic which is all their own, often to the author's surprise, and sometimes to his consternation. They are not merely pawns in his game, but accomplices, bound together by some mysterious vital harmony, acting in concert like the instruments of an orchestra. Suddenly they know better than I what to do. For it is the thing to be done which has brought them to life together, as a certain phrase calls up not only its own particular reply, but someone capable of uttering it.

Le Pain dur is the result of this kind of logic. Once the first principle is laid down, it applies to characters brought from all the corners of the globe. For all these fatherless children, this kind of deep organic need, the development of a principle which must have its consequences, has taken the place of free, intelligent, and filial obedience. The creatures I have imagined lack the counterbalance provided by the understanding of a general code outside themselves, which would have molded their actions according to that higher *music* spoken of in the passage from *Ecclesiasticus* which I quoted a moment ago. They become incapable of curbing, ruling, or verifying, as a singer verifies in his part, the secret impulses which spring from the very depths of their being; and these impulses move them like puppets, one by one, until at the end they are grouped in a kind of sinister tableau, a parable upside down.[19]

Later still—but we judged it best to take liberties with chronology —further attacks on *L'Otage* led Claudel to justify his conception of "historical drama." He did this briefly in a letter to Pierre Brisson on 9 June 1930:

Is the fable of *L'Otage* absurd? That is to say does it rest on impossible premises? Would it not be more correct to say that it is synthetic and stylized, and that it has brought into sharp relief a historical situation which we have often seen in a blurred state, simply by exaggerating it and clearing away from it all irrelevant events? *L'Otage* is the outcome of two facts, both authentic and both of undeniable human interest. The first is the captivity of the Pope. . . . The second is the downfall (not at all the right word) of noble families forced to put themselves in the hands of their former servants. . . . I have fused these two profoundly dramatic situations into one story, following the example of many great dramatists, and the reaction of the audience proves that I made no mistake.[20]

He wrote at greater length in *Le Figaro* for 29 October 1934:

On L'Otage

We see from the history of literature that there are two ways of treating historical drama.

The first, used by the great English and Spanish dramatists of the seventeenth century, is to choose a certain number of characteristic episodes which give the audience a vivid sense of opposing forces, of characters in conflict, of events building up and being resolved. This technique has been revived in the modern cinema, for example in that masterpiece of crudity, *The Private Life of Henry VIII*.

The conception of our own great classical tragedy is quite different. The Frenchman lives in valleys and loves horizons. Line, continuity, dignity are all-important to him. Rather than to feel, he likes to know and understand. He likes to see before him a complete and comprehensive whole, well constructed and composed, on which both eye and mind can take and keep hold. He likes things that last, things firmly fixed, that come to life as time flows past them, as when we follow the Rhône Valley and watch the double line of hills and mountains moving with us like a melody constantly broken and constantly renewed. In the same way tragedies like *Bérénice*, *Le Cid*, *Britannicus*, and *Polyeucte* move like a sort of insistent counterpoint. The individual passions of the characters mark a painful and more or less successful effort toward the solution or at least the clarification of a universal crisis or conflict of ideas. The play has done its work when it has found a compromise between the opposing forces which stem from necessity or duty; and its characters are enlisted for the solution of a problem far greater than themselves.

The second conception is that of *L'Otage*. . . .

I shall not try to justify the liberties which the author of *L'Otage* takes with historical truth. Drama has the same license as legend, and does the same work at less length. Reality is only a sketch which the artist has the right to complete. The signposts of history are few and uncertain, and it is the dramatist who shows us the road.

Protée

In 1919 Gheusi proposed putting on the *Oresteia* and *Protée* at the Théâtre du Gymnase. To Claudel's delight, the plans for the "satyr play" took shape fairly quickly, and since Sert, who had been approached about the sets and costumes, did not seem very enthusiastic, the poet sent Darius Milhaud full production notes from Copenhagen.[21]

27 October 1919

Yesterday I sent Francis a note in which I gave him two ideas for sets: either Larionov and Gontcharova, or all the hurly-burly of scenery being set up—sets half-painted.

I enclose an idea for the set, but I'm not really happy about it. Suggestion for the first scene:

We should create the impression of a fantastic island straight away. We could for example treat it in monochrome, using only yellow tones shading into red ochre.* We could have palm trees, with yellow trunks and yellow leaves, keeping only the relative depth of color. Costumes

---

* Another color range: pink, red, and silver.—P. C.

in the same color range from pale lemon to terra-cotta. One single costume to make a splash of contrast—Brindosier in a kind of tunic or nebris, with heavy diagonal black stripes, even on the sleeves, ending in a sort of pointed tail.

1. A monstrous clump of vegetation in shades of red, with a great spike of aloes in the center, treated violently and crudely.

2. Palm trees, the trunk pale gold and the leaves red-gold.

3. The Sea, shading from pale lemon to silver.

4. Small temple in a fantastic shape with a staircase: brown ochre.

5. Squat idols, Carthaginian or Aztec.

6. Another below in a niche.

7. A sky splashed with great curved egg-colored flames (Troy burning).

16 November 1919

The set for Protée must do several things at once for us:

From the point of view of *color*, it must be pleasant and satisfying to the eye, which has to look at it for quite a long time. The characters must never strike a discordant note, but must fit into the scene perfectly in both color and movement.

From the point of view of composition, it must give a fanciful, fantastic impression, a little fey. Proteus' island in all its aspects must always be an island of fancy.

It is very important that a vast stretch of grayish boards should not kill the general effect of color. The stage should be covered with a carpet in a shade to harmonize with the rest.

Another difficulty is the great empty space formed by the backcloth, so I have thought of various devices to bring it to life.

*First scene:**
Monochrome, yellow on yellow.

Every shade of yellow from saffron to ochre. Scenery consisting of date palms rather like Latour's famous palm. They must not be flat cutouts, but three-dimensional. One is straight, the other, right, is leaning over. On the right, staircase and terrace in ochre, decorated with small squat idols in Aztec or Carthaginian style. At the bottom, in a little

* The rather confused drawing accompanying these notes could not be reproduced. It is, on the whole, a repetition of the one reproduced in the preceding letter.

niche, an idol of the same kind. In the background, great curved flames symbolizing the burning of Troy. (A very blurred background, no violent contrast.) An the right an exotic yellow and red plant from which rises a very tall stem with flowers like silver bells. Menelaus' sail behind the little temple on the right. In the sky, right, a medallion with the Dioscuri, Helen's brothers, very lightly sketched in pale blue.

(Do not forget the huge date palm flower in the center—both beautiful and decorative.)

Brindosier, with her shrimp-colored (?) tunic with wide black diagonal stripes (perhaps also sleeves) will make a vivid splash of color in all this. Bare feet, or sandals fastened with yellow ribbons.

Menelaus I rather think should have bare feet, striped trousers, a red shirt with sleeves rolled up, and a Grecian helmet covering his whole face. A bow in his hand (?).

Helen in full evening dress, modern, black, low-cut, with bracelets and an enormous black hat with huge feathers.

We shall have to experiment with combinations of yellow shades, darkening to ochre, playing round a black center, until we find something completely satisfying to the eye.

Decide on the color of the stage carpeting (very important) perhaps with geometrical designs.

—Yellow seems absolutely right for a play in which Menelaus is the protagonist.*

Second scene (p. 119)**

On the right, a mass of spiky rocks among which seals and porpoises are cutting all sorts of capers.

Left, the entrance of a vast cavern in the shape of a dragon's mouth (rather in the Italian Renaissance style) with the top part bronze-green and the lips and gums pink. The whole of the inside of the jaw decorated with pennons. The interior of the cave filled with groceries, particularly

---

* In a separate note, difficult to date exactly, Claudel describes his characters as follows:
  "*Costumes*:
  Menelaus, cuirass of cowhide with the hair still on, belt, voluminous black cape, fringes.
  Helen and Brindosier, each with dress and cloak, four different reds. Red cloak with black spots as big as dinner plates."
** The rather confused sketch could not be reproduced, but the lines that follow describe it fairly accurately.

canned goods—cans in silver and smoked gold—and lit by electric light. In the background is the entrance to the tunnel which can be lit with red. On the left a table with a green cloth like the ones used for the baccalaureate examination. The six pots of tobacco plants neatly arranged on it. Menelaus and Helen, entering from the orchestra by a small flight of steps, hide behind it. The convex bathtub is painted a hideous pink with pretty curving patterns in indigo. Above it, half of a dismantled Great Wheel with its cars hanging, looking like half a dandelion clock, miserably abandoned by a bankrupt contractor. On the right, a sky in red and indigo and a sea ultramarine blue. Long trails of pink clouds, stylized in the Japanese manner. On each side of the nostrils, moustaches formed by spiky tufts of aloes. Flight of steps going toward Proteus, up which the seals are crawling. For the screen at the end we could use a frame in which the arithmetic problems Proteus gives his flock would appear (???)—Clothesline inside the cave with all kinds of multicolored rags drying on it (??).

For Milhaud

Will the music be enough to fill the time we need for the change of scene?

Further thoughts on Scene I

I suggest the center palm tree could have a live actor in it? It could give rise to some quite good comic business. The tree could be seen to swing round and the leaves to move. When Menelaus ties Helen to it (he never lets go of her—or else he ties her up, puts a stone on her, etc.) the palm tree moves and pulls her toward the open mouth without her even noticing it. Or she hangs her mirror on the trunk, and when she looks for it, the tree has moved and it is around the other side, etc. This business could fill the whole of the first scene. Instead of the Gemini in the medallion, we could perhaps have Jupiter with the thunderbolt and Menelaus could address his objurgations to him (?).

2nd scene

The sea and the sky should not be unbroken, but indicated by a heavy band and by a few streaks perhaps.

Proteus. Singlet of coarse cotton in garish pink like a circus strong man. Skintight.
Menelaus. As in the first act.
Brindosier (?).
(A live parrot on a perch?)

3rd scene

Shown in detail—The difficulty is that the scene at the beginning suggests night, while the rest of the act has more of an afternoon atmosphere.
1. Pink coral grotto.*
2. Mythological medallions. . . .
3. Parapet and bench parallel with the sea. Porphyry, speckled pink and black.
4. Yellowish-pink obelisk.
5. Bench at the foot of the obelisk.
6. Gap through which the sea and the Satyrs' boat can be seen.
7. The sun-chariot and Apollo in unrelieved black . . . in a circle surrounded by rays.
8. Vines and creepers laden with gourds and great bunches of fruit. Green and yellow.
9. The sky blue (very clear), the sea blood-red.
10. The Satyrs' boat with tan-colored sail. Not the same as in the following scene, but smaller. . . .
Some way of throwing the shadow of the obelisk and the vine on the stage.
Red light like the setting sun for the poetic scene between Menelaus and the two Helens.

4th scene

Fixed, stylized waves, Prussian blue with white crests.
Left, a purple-black island like the finger of God.
Right, Proteus' island, dancing and whirling madly in time with the music—up to the moment when it rises up into the sky (if possible).
This scene begins on page 190.

* The different parts of the set are numbered from left to right in a drawing that accompanied these notes. The drawing is too confused to be reproduced.

5. There will be an interval, as short as possible, for change of scene. M. Gheusi will decide on the proportion of speech to music. There is no reason why speech should not continue even when the music is at full strength. Perhaps a few short moments of silence would also do no harm.

Menelaus could have a naval officer's cap and a telescope.

Proteus's boat*

1. The eyes.
2. Moustaches.
3. Khaki neck with a ridge up the middle.
4. Wings, or fins, which the boat flaps gracefully along its own sides.
5. Black tarred part of boat with something like teeth under the keel.
6. Green part (coarse green).
7. Mast with sails and rigging extremely tangled.
8. Tiller in the shape of an enormous wriggling fishtail.
9. Rowers and oars.

Milhaud

See my letter in which I explain how the boat dances, rising and falling in time with the music. The boat must be big.

Claudel does in fact describe this "dance" in a letter of 22 July:

In the foreground a boat with the Satyrs rowing frenziedly but remaining in the same place—The landscape moves, as in cinemas. Below, stylized waves.
When the rowers say

Il lui faut
aut
aut

at each aut the ship goes up a little, and it rises still more on the following line

Il lui faut . . .

and falls back on

. . . le médecin.

* Claudel's drawing could not be reproduced and is, indeed, very difficult to understand. The boat must be intended as some kind of monster.

During this time the island—which, remember, is a floating one—
is dancing joyously, and we can even imagine it dancing in time—for
example it might bob to left and right on each *aut*
Until Iris takes it up to heaven.
That should be underlined by the music.

Gheusi very soon left this theatre, without having put on any of
Claudel's plays.

L'Homme et son désir

At the beginning of 1917 Claudel left for Brazil. At Rio de Janeiro he saw Nijinsky dance and later met him.[22]

Nijinsky appeared.

I have never had much taste for the conventional art of ballet as it is practiced, often with soulless perfection, by many subsidized companies, or by the sinister Pavlova. I don't like it any more than I do the tricks of singers and violinists. Beauty is something you rarely find when you are looking for it. It is natural that false artists, exasperated by the glorious fickleness of inspiration, should try to replace it with a formula, superstitiously followed, or with the sort of desperately hard work which Latin mockingly calls *improbus*. But you can't make a silk purse from a sow's ear, and grace was never won by merit. So I was one of those who could appreciate only the Oriental style of dancing, in which the feet scarcely ever leave the ground; it is like a speech, each phrase of which starts from the solar plexus, and as the body turns to face every point on the circumference of a circle, the phrase ripples through the limbs to the fingertips—a complete movement, slowly unfolding or suddenly flashing into flame. Or else it is the tireless visual response to a phrase taken up and repeated a hundred times by the flute and the drum.

Nijinsky's contribution was different. At last contact with the earth was broken! He gave us the leap, the victory of breath control over gravity. As the actor or singer spreads his arms simply to broaden the movement of his chest as the air fills it, so the dancer's inspiration, and that desire for life that is in all of us, are enough to lift him from the ground, which becomes no more than a springboard under his feet! The spirit rules the body, uses it, and soars like a great bird to meet a glorious defeat. The dancer falls back, like a king stepping down from his throne, and soars again, like an eagle, both the arrow and the bow that fires it. For a second the soul bears the body aloft, the earthly garment becomes flame, and the flesh melts into an ecstasy! He flashes across the stage like lightning and has scarce time to turn before he is back on us again like a thunderbolt. He is the greatest human creation, lyricism incarnate, standing like a god among the jerking puppets that we are. He paints our passions on the canvas of Eternity, he takes our most misused gestures, as Virgil took our words and images, and transports them into the blissful realm of all that is intelligent, powerful, and ethereal. Even in Scheherazade, when the negro curves for an instant like a spring, and, with those charmed hands which are not hands but lips, a greedy tongue and even a mind, touches, or rather, measures, draws, and creates an ideal body around the half-hidden body of the beautiful woman, the gesture, which could have been lewd, takes on an indescribable dignity and grandeur. . . .

Once Nijinsky consented to come with me to the Legation, and I could look at him closely. He walked as tigers walk; it was not the shifting of a dead weight from one foot to the other, but all the complex of muscles and nerves moving buoyantly, as a wing moves in the air, in a body which was not a mere trunk or a statue, but the perfect organ of power and movement. Every tiny gesture, as for example when he turned his face toward us and his small head swung round suddenly on his long neck, was accomplished gloriously, with a vivacity both fierce and sweet, and at the same time an overwhelming authority. Even in repose, he seemed to be dancing imperceptibly.

> The outcome of this meeting was the ballet *L'Homme et son désir*, written in the following weeks. It was performed in June 1921, and Claudel wrote an introduction to it in *La Danse:*

L'Homme et son désir is the fruit of the collaboration of three friends who, during the year 1917, held a picnic of ideas, music and design every Sunday in the Serra above Rio de Janeiro. This little drama in movement had its birth in the atmosphere of the Brazilian forest which, in its vast uniformity, seemed like an element in which we were immersed. It is most strange at night, when it begins to be filled with movement, cries, and gleams of light; and it is one such night that we are trying to show in our poem. We have not tried to reproduce its inextricable tangle with photographic accuracy. We have simply spread it like a carpet—violet, green, and blue—around the central blackness on the four tiers of our stage. This stage appears vertical to the eye, like a picture, or a book being read. It is, if you like, a page of music in which each action is written on a different stave. The Hours of Night, all in black with gilded headdresses, move one by one along the topmost ridge. Below, the Moon, led across the sky by a cloud, like a servant walking before a great lady. At the very bottom, in the waters of the vast primeval swamp, the Reflection of the Moon and her Servant follows the measured walk of the celestial pair. The drama proper takes place on the platform halfway between heaven and earth. And the principal character is Man in the grip of primeval powers, robbed by Night and Sleep of both face and name. He enters led by two women, identical in their veils, who confuse him by turning him round and round like a child blindfolded for a game. One is Image and the other Desire, one is Memory and other Illusion. Both mock him for a while, then disappear.

He remains there, standing with outstretched arms, sleeping in the brilliance of the tropical moon, like a man drowned in deep waters. And all the animals, all the noises of the eternal forest come out of the orchestra to watch him and din in his ears: the Bells and the Panpipes, the Strings and the Cymbals.

The man begins to move in his dream, and to dance. And his dance is the age old dance of nostalgia, Desire and Exile, the dance of captives and deserted lovers, of those insomniacs who pace in a fever from one end to the other of their verandah, of caged beasts that fling themselves and fling themselves again—and again, and again—upon the impassable bars. Sometimes a hand from behind pulls him back, sometimes a fragrance which saps all vitality. The theme of obsession becomes more and more violent and frenzied, and then, at the darkest of the dark hours before the dawn, one of the women returns, and circles round the man as though fascinated. Is this a dead woman? or a live one? The sleeper grasps the corner of her veil; she whirls round him and her veil unwinds until he is wrapped around like a chrysalis, and she is almost naked—and then, joined by the last wisp of stuff, very like that of our dreams, the woman puts her hand on his face and both move away to the side of the stage.

Of the Moon and her attendant all we see is the reflection, down below.

The black Hours have ceased to file past, and the first white Hours appear.

The allusion to the "verandah" is a warning bell to anyone interested in Claudel. It recalls painful memories of Foochow, a poem from *Connaissance de l'est*, and above all a passage from *Le Soulier de satin:*

Let me explain myself! Let me free myself from these tangled threads of thought! Let me unfold, for all to see, that web I wove through long nights, thrown from one wall to the other of that bitter verandah like a shuttle in the hands of the dark Fates.

This comparison shows that Claudel tried to find, in movement and dance, the exact equivalent of the poetic image.

He wrote, as we know, other plots for ballets (he preferred to call them mime plays): *Le Femme et son ombre, Le Peuple des hommes cassés.* The first has a theme very like that of *L'Homme et son désir,* and the effects sought after are identical down to minor details: "Here *La Femme et son ombre* is to be given at the Theatre Imperial, with Japanese music. I used the idea of the moon and its reflection, but in an improved form" (letter to Milhaud, 6th January 1922). The same atmosphere, rarely achieved in the theatre, is present in both; Claudel tried to recapture it in *L'Ours et la lune* by the use of marionettes, and found it hard to give up a scene in *Le Soulier de satin* in which it was essential: that of the double Shadow.

But in the two last ballets, the influence of the Japanese theatre was already perceptible.

The Japanese Theatre

There is no need for commentaries here; the texts are enough. Claudel, who on arrival in Japan was immediately attracted by their theatre in all its forms, appears to have written these comments after *Le Soulier de satin* was finished. On 23 April 1926, he wrote to Copeau, "I am working hard, particularly on studies of the Japanese theatre in its different forms."[23]

Bugaku

Old China is dead, but its faint reflection still glimmers over its neighbor countries, once tinged with its madness: in Annam, the ceremonial costumes of the mandarins, which are still those of the Ming dynasty; in Korea, the Confucian orchestra of bells and thin plates of jade; in Japan the company of singers and dancers at the Imperial court who hand down from father to son the traditions of the Tang period. I have been able to observe them—alas!—only twice, when the Prince of Wales came to visit His Majesty. The orchestra consists of flutes and mouth-blown organs with slender pipes, a few mandoras, a big drum in the middle and small gongs at the ends. Here the object of the music is not, as it is elsewhere, to depict movement, or illustrate the action of the play. It is there to make us aware of eternal time, that indivisible presence outside ourselves. There are sustained notes of indefinite length, placed one above the other like geological "horizons," and as one stops, the others immediately become clearer. Over this a few plucked notes, a heavy stroke that thunders or crashes, a metallic noise, accentuate those long, ever-receding sounds.

The first drama we see is a Korean dance, the battle of the male and female Dragons. They are not human figures so much as an exaltation of veils, one red, the other white, with masks of Elements and Passions, and they hold in their fingers short silver wands which are the line of the shining water. And we see the swirling of vapor slowly rising, expanding, contracting, curling in wisps or falling to lick the ground like a hydra; we see the immense beings irresolute between earth and heaven, unable to tear themselves away from either, drawn to one by gravity and to the other by light, the many-shaped equilibrium between spirit and water, the dialogue of steam and condensation, water rising into the sky and falling again! But four figures have now come forward with great ceremony, each very precisely after a pause, his stature and dress exactly like the one before him. They had taken up their positions at the four corners of the stage. They are like the Four Guardians of the old temples, or, more exactly, like the stone warriors standing before classical tombs. They are the demigods, the heroes of the days of the Empty Earth, the leaders of hordes, the founders of kingdoms, the lords sung by the Shi King. The programme says vaguely, *Spring Festival*. But this is something quite different from the gay flowering of the cherry trees in our little garden. The music has become cruel, assailing the mind like an intermittent wind that pierces you to the bone, like the fierce sun that melts the ice, like an acid greenness, or a bitter sap, and always that long, long note, as far as the mind can reach! The vision of the Yellow Earth coming out of the desert of Oigour! an altar to God in the curve of the Hwang-ho, those broad valleys strewn with the bones of the fossil creation, scraped and planed by the movement of the glaciers. And now the four God-Men are facing each other. Each with a wide sweep of the hands fixes the horizon, describes the land, takes possession of it, measuring it with the stately unfolding of his outstretched arms, and affirms before heaven his right to this land, which was *res nullius*, belonging to no one. Other dances imitate the hunt or the forge; here we see the sacred ceremony of the Measuring, a religious and geometric rite. There is a reason for every detail of it—the number of steps, the foot identified with its own footprint, the great backward kick which takes possession of the surface, the circle drawn by the leg, the simultaneous movement to the center and return to the four cardinal points, and the triumphant end to the calculations, which here, in this holy place, taking slopes and contours into account, finally join angles and radii. It remains only to make the sacrifice to the sound of the Psalm of Ham.

Bunraku

This is the name of the puppet theatre of Osaka, from which comes modern drama, called *Kabuki*.

A puppet is the complete animated likeness, not only of the face, but of the limbs and the whole body. A living doll, a tiny man in our hands, a concentration of movement. A puppet is not, like a human actor, held captive by its own weight. It has no contact with earth, and moves with equal ease in all dimensions. It floats in an intangible element like a drawing in an empty space. Its life is in its center, and its four limbs and head, spread out like rays around it, are merely its elements of expression. It is a talking star, untouchable. The Japanese have not tried to make it walk; that is impossible, for it does not belong to the earth, but stands on an invisible stalk and turns its mocking face to every side. Legs and feet are not simply means of progress or support, but the instrument of every attitude, walk, and witty contortion, expressing anxiety, eagerness, resistance, defiance, weariness, awakening, and the wish to go or stay. Look—we'll lift him up so that you can see him! Look at that funny little man—he can do anything! Look at this lady and gentleman in the air—a whole slice of life at the end of a stick! And behind—it's so amusing to keep well hidden and make someone come to life; to create that little doll that goes in at the eyes of every spectator to strut and posture in his mind! In all those rows of motionless people only this little goblin moves, like the wild elfish soul of all of them. They gaze at him like children, and he sparkles like a little firecracker!

The Japanese puppet is not one of those that have nothing but a man's hand for body and soul. Nor do they dangle feebly at the end of strings, like someone dropped and caught up again by an uncertain fate. The puppeteer works them close to his body, heart to heart, and they spring so hard that you almost expect them to escape. There is always more than one puppeteer—there are two, sometimes three. They are bodiless and faceless, being dressed in a close-fitting black garment, with black-covered hands and face. The puppet is the collective soul of this wisp of shadow, this group of conspirators whose very existence one forgets. All we can see, like the hatching around a design, is this kind of black slime against which the majestic or frantic little lord stands out in his red and white or golden garments. It is a dialogue of two stars, each with its invisible train behind it.

On the right, squatting on a kind of platform, between two candles, there are two men in special costume, the narrator and the man who leads the audience's emotional reactions. The first has in front of him a lectern holding the book, and the wooden actors in the midst of the blackness obey, not hands and fingers as they do with us, but a secret conspiracy of hearts chiming with what he says. A strange Something breaks away from the book and borrows its language. These are not interpreters; they are the words themselves. The second man holds the long-necked Japanese guitar, the white catskin *shamisen*, on which from time to time he plucks a few notes with an ivory plectrum. The sound is probably rather like that of the classical lyre. But he is also a whole choir on his own. He may not speak, he may only moan and wail and utter those wordless animal noises which come directly from the chest when the breath is stopped by our various natural valves and reeds. He registers inquiry, joy, anxiety, suffering, desire, anger, fear, suspicion, and thought. He groans, weeps, mocks, abuses, insinuates, rages, roars, and caresses. His job is to stir up the audience's emotions. He is himself a whole public with his "oh's" and "ah's."* He has everything except speech.

Letter To Professor Miyajima

Tokyo, 17 November 1926

My dear Miyajima,

I have read with great interest your studies on the magnificent art of Japanese puppetry as practiced at the Bunraku theatre at Osaka. You know my admiration for it, and I am grateful to you for the opportunity to put it into words. The living actor, whatever his talent, always brings into the play an unwelcome intrusive element, a sort of hangover from everyday life. He is always a man dressed up. But the puppet has no life or movement beyond what springs from the action. The story itself awakens it, like a shade brought to life by telling it all that it has done, so that gradually it becomes, no longer a memory, but a presence. It is not an actor speaking, but speech acting. This wooden figure is the perfect example of personification, hovering over the uncertain dividing line between words and action. The audience, watching it, sees all that the narrator is saying, supported by the *shamisen*, that instrument which vibrates as though the hearer's own nerves were plucked, and by the colleague at his side whose cries and groans translate not only the

* There is an expression in Japanese literature: "To know the *Ah-ness* of things" (*mono no aware woshiru*) which means "that which makes us say AH!"—P. C.

emotion of the scene, but the striving for life of the imaginary being. The puppet is like a ghost. Its feet are never on the ground. No one touches it, and it can touch nothing. All its life and movement comes from the mysterious assembly of puppeteers behind it, sometimes masked, sometimes not. Its fate is governed by the collective mind of which it is the expression. The reality has been so skillfully apportioned that the story unfolds entirely in the imagination, without any unwanted material help. *Jorari* reaches by different means the same results as *Nō*.

I hope as many as possible of my compatriots will see this moving performance.

Nō

In drama something happens, but in Nō drama someone happens. It is rather like the door which appeared in the early days of Greek theatre as a means of communication through the wall with the invisible world behind, and in which the characters of the *Oresteia* appeared one by one. Here the stage is in two parts, the road or bridge, and the platform. The bridge is a long covered gallery attached to the back wall and divided by vertical supports into three equal parts. The platform is of wood,* polished like a mirror and framed by four columns holding up a roof. It is on the right side of the hall and projects at an angle into the audience. This arrangement is essential. The show is not being presented to a half-hidden public ready to lose itself in the action on the stage. We do not see a play on one side and an audience on the other, separated by the drama's make-believe as if by a flame-filled chasm. They intermingle one with the other, so that from our point of view the action unfolds laterally and on two levels, with which each member of the audience, according to his seat, makes his own personal geometric figures, as his eye and ear receive impressions at different angles. Everything happens within the audience, which feels both involved and remote at the same time. Even when the solemn figures have ceased to move along the bridge, it is still a place for majestic entrances and exits, and the platform, beneath its canopy, is like the pavilions of coral

---

* Under this platform a certain number of large earthenware jars are buried in the earth with their mouths uncovered to increase the sonority of the boards, which are always trodden by bare feet. To entice the sun goddess Amaterasu out of the cave in which she has taken refuge, the terrible Ama-no-uzume dances on an upturned barrel.—P. C.

and cinnabar in Chinese paintings, in which blessed souls in sea-green and azure robes make merry above the clouds; it speaks perpetually of a presence or an absence.

To right and left, on wood the color of fresh butter, green bamboos have been painted and, on the back panel, a tall pine. That is all we need to bring nature into the play.

Events take place in this order:

First come the musicians and the men of the chorus, with small, gliding steps. The musicians station themselves at the back of the plat-form in a section marked out for them by a change in the pattern of the floor, called the *Koza*. There is a flute, and two double-headed drums shaped like hourglasses, a small one slung over the right shoulder and a larger one held on the left knee, which give a sort of sharp crack when struck violently with the fingers held flat. For the entrances of gods, demons, and ghosts there is a drum played with sticks, and that is all. The percussion instruments are there to give rhythm and move-ment, and the dismal flute is the voice of the passing hours and moments, sounding in counterpoint to the voices of the actors. The musicians often add prolonged howls on two notes, one deep, the other shrill. This gives a strange dramatic impression of space and remote-ness, like the noises of the countryside at night, the formless calls of nature. Or perhaps it is the cry of an animal groping toward speech and always failing to reach it, a despairing effort, painful and vague.

The chorus takes no part in the action, but merely adds an impersonal commentary. It tells what has gone before, describes the scene, de-velops the theme, and explains the characters. It replies to the actors in poetry and song, it dreams and murmurs, squatting by the side of the speaking Statue.

There are only two characters in Nō drama, the *Waki* and the *Shite*. Each of these may or may not be accompanied by one or more *Tzure*, attendants, servants, advisers, or shadows, whose function is to add pomp and ceremony.

The *Waki* is the one who watches and waits, whose reason for com-ing is to wait. He has no mask, for he is a man. First comes the music as though preparing the way, then the heavy brocade curtain rises, we see him pass through the three openings in the gallery one by one, and then he is on the stage, turning his face slowly toward us, as though offering it. He begins usually by speaking two lines of verse, the first of which is repeated twice, and the chorus softly, as though to itself, repeats the sentence three times. Then, in a long speech, in which each step, a five-syllable followed by a seven-syllable line, seems to leave time for its contemplation, he proclaims who he is, and the road he has traveled. He is, for example, a monk who has explored the regions of the Underworld to bring back the dead concubine of a despairing Emperor. Or a madwoman wandering across the deserted land in search of her dead son. For the sex of the figure engulfed in those flowing robes does not matter—only his function. Then the *Waki*, with or without his escort, goes and sits at the foot of the front right-hand pillar which is his special place, and, his eyes fixed on the entrance, he waits.

He waits and someone appears.

God, hero, hermit, ghost, or demon, the *Shite* is always the ambassador of the Unknown, and so wears a mask. This is something secret, something hidden, which comes to the *Waki* to be revealed. His walk and movements depend on that gaze which drew him thither and keeps him chained to an imaginary earth. Here is the betrayed woman whose ghost, step by step, draws nearer to her murderer. For a whole long hour he keeps his eyes fixed on her; the whole audience is watching him, and he must not bat an eyelid. Here is the soul of the child Atsumori in the form of a reaper, and only the magic flute reveals who he is. The *Waki* asks questions, the *Shite* replies, and the choir comments, weaving a hedge of words and images around this tragic visitor who, beneath his mask, brings the terror of the unknown to the man who has called him up.

Then comes the interlude, and a passerby, in a conversational tone, asks the *Waki* for explanations, or gives them in a down-to-earth manner.

And the second part of the Nō play begins. The *Waki* has finished his part, and is now a mere onlooker. The *Shite* who had retired for a moment reappears. He has emerged from death, formlessness, or oblivion. He has changed his costume, sometimes his shape. Sometimes he is even a different person, and the one in the first half was simply his herald, his shell, or his shadow. Now the whole stage is his, and he takes possession of it and of all that is thereon. Part of that life of which he was the origin or the expression has awakened with him and fills with its invisible presence the Pavilion that sleeps in the middle of the Lake of Dreams. With a wave of his magic fan he has swept away the Present like a vapor, and with the slow beating of that mysterious wing he has commanded things past to rise around him. With the magic of a word that fades as another follows it, the garden of the underworld has taken shape in its murmuring ashes. The *Shite* no longer speaks. In a few words, a few melodic phrases, he provides themes, invitations, impulses, and the chorus, in his place, describes his position, both physical and moral, in a sort of impersonal chant. He walks to and fro, affirms, testifies, develops, acts, and shows by his changes of attitude and direction all the vicissitudes of this somnambulistic play. By an amazing paradox, the sentiment is not within the actor, but the actor within the sentiment. He acts out his own thought before us, and bears witness to his own expression.

The whole thing gives the impression of a dream which could be destroyed in a moment by too abrupt a movement, or one alien to the convention. It is essential that the actors' attention should not wander for a moment. They must move in a kind of trance, and the arm they raise even to weep or to kill must be leaden with sleep.* Every gesture springs from a kind of hypnosis, in harmony with the music—the inexhaustible flood of our grief, rising and falling—and with the chorus which is our memory. The actor does not seem to rest on the ground, and his steps are not the usual struggle against gravity. He glides over the shining surface, with no effort but the slight movement of his toes. It seems as though with each gesture he has to overcome not only gravity and the folds of the immense garment, but death itself; the gesture is the slow copy in eternity of a dead passion. It is life brought back from the Shades and mirrored in our mind's eye. We stand before ourselves, in the bitterness of our desire, our pain, our madness. We see each of our actions frozen in immobility, and nothing is left of movement but its meaning. Like a teacher repeating and explaining, someone is slowly reproducing our past acts before our eyes, so that now we can understand how every one of our poor random gestures was the unconscious imitation of some eternal attitude. It is as though a statue took shape for a moment in front of us. There is such tenderness in the hand which a husband lays on his loved one's shoulder as he passes, without even glancing at her; and the banal attitude of grief we see in every illustrated paper takes on a depth of meaning when the movement is slow and precise. It is a weight, the weight of sorrow, painfully

---

* A lord had told his fencing master to watch a certain famous Nō actor and to run him through with his sword if his attention should wander enough to leave him undefended even for an instant. At the end of the play, the swordsman owned himself beaten, but declared that the actor had left himself open for a fraction of a second. The cause was a grain of sand on the spotless mirror of the stage—P. C.

lifted; it is a cup raised to the lips, the longing to hide, the mirror in which we see our reflection with despair; it is our final end, there, for us to see.

The invention of Nō drama is more or less contemporary with that of the tea ceremony, and they are both the expression of the same spirit, that of actions carried out so precisely that they are perfect. Nō drama is still enthusiastically practiced by the cultured classes of Japanese society, as it was in the days of *Bushido*. I have seen a civil engineer, a member of the House of Peers, dancing with talent the part of the Willow Spirit, and the director of the School of Art told me that he had been studying the drum for two years. Its value is not only artistic and religious, but educational as well. It teaches both actor and spectator the importance of gesture, the art of controlling one's thoughts, words and movements, as well as patience, concentration, and decorum; for Nō drama, taken in a certain way, is less a play than a judgment at the hands of a tribunal of exacting enthusiasts.

If I were sufficiently knowledgeable, I think I should have much to say about the actor's delivery, and about the verse, which seems to consist entirely of a long line followed by a short one. This gives a quality of deliberation to the speeches; an incomplete idea is put forward, and then completed, as though the words stopped to let the thought catch up.* The Japanese language also admits of long smooth sentences, flowing like ribbons, without punctuation, in which the same word can be both subject and complement at the same time, fanning out into a whole sheaf of images and ideas.**

There remains the costume, and most particularly the Sleeve, the Mask, and the Fan.

The function of the costume is to give the proportions another

---

* "Probably the authors of the Nō plays were satisfied with the alternation of long and short lines, rather than a definite number of syllables. They were, of course, helped by the music, and provided the sense of the recitative was not hindered, they seem to have enjoyed a certain liberty with regard to the number of syllables" (Nöel Péri, *Cinq Nō*).—P. C.

** "The word *pivot*, a word having two significations, serves as a species of hinge on which two doors turn, so that while the first part of the poetical phrase has no logical end, the latter part has no logical beginning. They run into each other, and the sentence does not have a possible construction. For the European reader such a punning invention will doubtless seem the height of misapplied ingenuity. But as a matter of fact the impression produced by these linked verses is delightful in the extreme, passing as they do before the reader like a series of dissolving views, vague, graceful, and suggestive" (Chamberlain, *The Classical Poetry of the Japanese*).—P. C.

dimension and to replace lines by surfaces. In the old Japanese court costume, each leg had its own silken robe, and the lords of olden time dragged a long train behind each foot. Each was a procession on his own. But with his great sleeves the actor can build his own shape, according to the idea of himself he wishes to produce. He has more than words to use; in his rich plumage he wheels, explodes, turns, shimmers, and the light playing over him brings out all kinds of subtle shades and reflections. We thrill as he walks down the long gallery to speak to us in that language of fire and peonies, of jewels and leaves. The hand has a hundred ways of coming out of the sleeve to stretch out toward life, or to refuse a request or discourage curiosity. As the arm moves, every action it has done or is about to do hangs from it like a heavy, empty trophy. The *Shite* appears before the eyes of the *Waki*, swelling and unfolding to the whole span of his arms and shoulders; this, together with the dazzling gold of his fan, makes him so splendid, so wrapped in color and light, that he seems to expand before our gaze, as though he were about to disappear in his own apotheosis. Or he moves both arms to right and left with a strange inevitability as though preparing to catch us in his fatal net. And in the admirable play *Hagoromo*, which is acted in the clear January cold, we see the Angel, having won back her consecrated robe, holding curved above her head one beautiful arm and literally rising to Heaven in a column of snow and gold.

At the same time of year, as a sort of salute to the New Year, another Nō play is acted—a very old and interesting one called *Okina*. It is religious in character, and the actor who plays the main part prepares for it by a day of purification and fasting. The performance takes place at sunrise and begins with a kind of procession in which the priest—for that is what he is—ceremoniously carries in his arms a gold-lacquered box from which, after the most magnificent obeisance I have ever seen, he brings out the mask of an old man (the one which was used that day is the original, kept for centuries in one of the four great families responsible for handing on the Nō traditions, the Hosho family). The mask is donned and the ritual begins. As far as I could understand, it is a sort of sacred progress through the world of nature, purifying and renewing. The man's two hands appear to be occupied in all sorts of work, and his foot, with magnificent pride, strikes the earth (two light blows and one heavy) to take possession of it with its waters and its crops. And as I watched the movements of this character on the stage, no longer a man, but appointed by the people to be temporarily a god or an angel, I wondered whether this costume and mask might not be a kind of disguise. Nature is a wild thing, terrified by man and his intelligence; in order to tame her, to induce her to work peacefully with us, might we not have to imitate the hunter who turns himself into an animal or a bush to approach his prey? But the mask has the same function throughout Nō drama—to cut the character off from the present time, and to keep the outward form of the passion he expresses, in the age of which he is the symbol and the historic or legendary event which he helped to make. Between him and us, between the *Shite* and the *Waki*, is this hard unalterable mask, the final seal of something that can no longer be changed. The old Japanese expression was not to "carve" but to "strike" a mask. The past, or a dream, comes to life for a moment and answers our questions, but does not sever the threads which bind it to the other world, does not take off that face which exists only to hide what is behind it. The actor is hidden, and the more he shows himself, the more he shows the thing that hides him.

Above the mask is the helmet, the headdress, the crest, lifting the character above the common level and keeping him in proportion with his flowing costume. The Nō wardrobe has an incredible variety of headdresses, from flowers, tiaras, crowns and capes, to a tiger, or a lion, a stork, a dragon. It is the character's mark, his standard, his title, the thing in whose name he comes.

The ancient Chinese or Korean statues, imitated later by the Japanese, hold between their hands a slip of wood, the purpose of which was to focus the eyes and the mind and thus keep the will firm and unwavering. It was to the thinker what the sword is to the fencer, extending outside his body the line of convergence of all his forces, behind which he is alert and safe.* Later this straight line opened to become both an angle and a surface at the same time—angles in every direction, joined and measured as they spring from the fingers, and a surface that delicately separates what is above from what is below, like a wing whose beating shows every hesitation of a spirit ever ready to stop dead or flee. This is the Fan, at once triangle and semicircle, horizontal and vertical, instrument of all relationships, which are visible when it is open, and invisible when it is closed. Spoke by spoke, it opens and closes like a thought or plan which by turns unfolds, half reveals itself, shrinks into itself again, and becomes as straight and stiff as an injunction. And the words of the play unfold too, and from their narrow

---

* An iron fan was part of the panoply of the ancient Japanese warriors.—P. C.

rectangle become a whole panorama of writing, bright with color. And when we see the fan in the hand of that master of dreams, the Nō actor, perpetually before us, we naturally see it as a scepter and a veil at the same time. It is the only moving thing on that statue, and vibrates in the hand like human foliage. As I have said, it is like a wing, mimicking the quivering thoughts that drop to earth and rise again to wheel and hover. It is the splash of golden light that builds a rainbow from the robes, that beats slowly on the heart, that moves for the motionless face. It is an opened flower, a flame in the hand, a dart, the horizon of thought, the vibration of the soul. When the Reed-Cutter, in the play of the same name, finds his lost wife after a long separation, their emotion is seen only in the quivering of two fans that mingle their breath for an instant.

Kabuki

"They cry too much up there!" said the man under the stage, "and I'm too tenderhearted. Even when plays begin quite reassuringly, there's always something creeping in gradually, like when you're sitting in a draught and you feel uncomfortable from head to toe and you know that any minute you're going to sneeze. And here it comes! Somebody kills a child, or abandons a poor geisha, or the old gentleman who generally plays young girls sells his charms to the brothel keeper, or the faithful servant dies in agony. The whole audience starts sobbing, all their little noses buried in their little handkerchiefs, while on the stage they twist their great sleeves and do terrifying tricks with their eyebrows, the men masquerading as women yelp and pour with sweat, and horrible rumblings attack all those manly chests. To me, it was like an earthquake. I had to go out, my stomach couldn't stand it. Even when I had to play the hind legs of a cardboard horse, it caught up on me and made me shake my rider about like an apple tree. Every time I saw the expressions on that chap's face, there on the stage, with his book in front of him and the audience all seeing themselves in it, it used to catch me in the pit of the stomach.

"I decided to move down, and I'm very peaceful and philosophical here. I'm on the frontier between fiction and reality, and well protected from both of them. Up there a storm is raging, and the actors who have to feed it rush past me like thunderbolts, but down here in the depths all is quiet and I can smoke my pipe. Carry on, friends! The old gentleman-woman up there, who is just providing a shining example of submission to one's mother-in-law, and all the other virtues, doesn't suspect that two yards under his feet is the man who has the job of cutting his throat. For the moment this instrument of Fate is busy discussing the tram drivers' strike with me. Careful—in a moment he'll appear at the end of the *hana-michi!** I have the best place, at the back. Reinforcements pass from time to time, the actors come off, dripping with sweat, but in the wings and the dressing rooms it's as peaceful as a field hospital. The hairdresser tidies up the blue heads with their little pigtails and the shiny black wigs. Sets are being stacked and costumes hung up, someone is making glue, and someone is very gently tapping something; and someone puts a cup of tea beside the musician in his cage, who, his eye on the stage I can't see, and his stick raised, is getting ready to bang.**

"Sometimes one of the walking wounded, half himself and half his part, brings us news of the battle. But I like to be under the stage even better than the wings. I'm alone there, and happy. I look up into the tangle of beams and joists and see the rollers which turn the stage round, each with its vertical handle. It's full of tricks! I am watching the roots and the machinery of a play I shall never see."

* The *hana-michi*, or bridge across the whole theatre (sometimes there are two) is, with the revolving stage, one of the finest inventions of the Japanese theatre. It makes possible effects of surprise, as the actor comes upon the audience suddenly from behind; of distance, as it is outside the stage and begins a long way from it; of precessions; of arrivals and departures; of menace taking gradual shape. It is a bridge over our heads between the play and the deep storehouses of possibility —P. C.

** The Japanese theatre has solved perfectly the problem of music in the theatre. It must never compete with the action or alternate with it, like an item in a concert, but act as intermediary between play and audience. There are a few notes on the *shamisen* to attract or relax the attention, and to point from time to time the singing which is the natural reply of the poetry to the play, or of the flow of thought to the action. There are a few sudden strokes of the gong to herald violent episodes, or else solemn ones at well-spaced intervals, or a great thundering when called for. Sometimes there is a plaintive flute, and the whole is carried out freely and almost instinctively.—P. C.

Le Soulier de satin

Parts of the complete text are as good as a treatise on the theatre, especially the preface and the scenes of the Irrepressible and of the Actress.[24]

Since after all it's not quite impossible that all or part of the play may be performed one day ten or twenty years hence, we may as well begin with a few stage directions. The most carelessly daubed backcloth, or none at all, will do. The stagehands make any necessary alterations in full view of the public while the action is going on. There is no reason why the actors should not give a hand if need be. The actors in each scene appear before those in the preceding scene have finished speaking, and immediately get down to preparations for their scene. When anyone remembers, and provided that it does not get in the way of the movement, the stage directions can either be posted up or read by the stage manager or the actors themselves, who can take the necessary papers out of their pockets or pass them round. If they get them wrong, it does not matter. A rope that has got caught up, or a backcloth not pulled across properly, so that we can see a blank wall with the stagehands walking backward and forward, will give a wonderful effect. Everything must look temporary, slapdash, incoherent, improvised in wild enthusiasm. If possible, there should be occasional successes, for we must avoid montony even in disorder.

Order is reason's pleasure, but disorder is imagination's delight.

I shall take it that my play is being performed, for example, on Shrove Tuesday at four o'clock in the afternoon. I imagine a large theatre, warmed by an earlier show, invaded by the public, and full of chatter. Through the double doors we can hear the muffled noise of a well-fed orchestra playing in the foyer. In the theatre itself a reedy little orchestra is joyfully imitating the noises of the audience, conducting them and gradually giving them a sort of rhythm and shape.

The Announcer appears on the apron in front of the curtain. He is a sturdy, bearded fellow, and his plumed hat, the cane under his arm and the swordbelt which he has great difficulty in buckling, all come out of Velasquez at his most banal. He tries to speak, but every time he opens his mouth, while a tremendous preliminary uproar is going on in the audience, he is interrupted by a clash of cymbals, a silly tinkling bell, a strident trill on the fife, a rude remark on the bassoon, a giggle from the ocarina or a belch from the saxophone. Gradually it all piles up, then there is silence. All we hear is the big drum patiently going "boom-boom-boom," like Mme. Bartet rhythmically tapping the table with a resigned forefinger as she listens to the Count's reproaches. Beneath this is a pianissimo drum roll with an occasional forte, until the audience is more or less quiet.

The Announcer has a paper in his hand. He bangs hard on the ground with his cane, and announces:

THE SATIN SLIPPER
or
THE WORST MAY NEVER HAPPEN
A Spanish story in four days
SECOND DAY
Scene II
THE IRREPRESSIBLE, DOÑA HONORIA, DOÑA PROUHÈZE

General bustle. The music imitates the sound of a carpet being beaten, and raising an enormous cloud of dust. While the sets from the preceding scene are being dragged about, the Irrepressible *appears among the stage hands, ordering them about and jostling them like a circus clown.*

THE IRREPRESSIBLE, *twirling the tailor's yardstick and making passes like a toreador with the red material:* Come on, you churls—the audience is getting impatient! hurry up, please! Get a move on there! Take that out of the way! Let's have some space!

—"Churls" is a good stagey word. I ought to have waited for my costume. But I hadn't the patience to go on moldering in that dressing room where the author stuck me. The dresser came to the door twenty times, and each time she wanted somebody else, and there was I, left marking time on my chair in front of the mirror.

I'm too eager for them, I go too fast. In two strides we'd be at the end and the audience would be too delighted for words.

That's why the author keeps me in reserve, just in case, with a whole crowd of extras who tramp noisily through the attics of his imagination, and whose faces you never see.

But I can't be kept under so easily, I slip under the door like gas and explode in the middle of the room.

Watch out, we're off! I'm flying away on my magic bidet.

He mimes pedaling at full speed on an invisible bicycle.

We aren't at Cadiz any longer, we're in the Sierra Something-or-other, in the middle of one of those famous Catalonian forests.

A peak! And there's Don Rodrigo's castle! Don Rodrigo is here, in a very bad way. His wound is playing him up, I think he's going to die. . . . No, I'm wrong, he'll have to get better or the play would be over. Allow me to introduce Don Rodrigo's Mama.

Enter Doña Honoria

THE IRREPRESSIBLE *with a roar:* Stay where you are! Wait till I fetch you!

Damn you, who told you to come? Get out! Get out!

Exit Doña Honoria

Don Rodrigo's Mama, Doña Whatshername. . . . Will Honoria do?

—She *would* have to come in! I was just going to do you her portrait.

It's infuriating what happens to me. That's why I couldn't be a painter. My figures suddenly begin to exist before I've even sketched in their eyes.

Look! I'm drawing Doña Honoria.

He draws with a piece of chalk on the stage manager's back.

Well, before I've put in her earrings, she'll start putting her tongue out at me, and she'll float off this fellow's back like Marguerite from the head of Jupiter.

When I do a dog, I haven't finished his backside before he starts wagging his tail and runs off on three legs without waiting for his head.

Oh, well! You'll see for yourself in a moment.

He throws the chalk into the middle of the audience.

Now the morning sun has gone, it is late, and there is a beautiful moon.

He hums the beginning of the "Moonlight Sonata."

Hey, you up there! Let down the backcloths! Main floodlight on! Front spot, prompt side!

Now that we have the atmosphere we want, I ask your permission to bring on Doña Prouhèze. What a name! It almost makes her real!

Doña Prouhèze arrived here, in the costume you have seen, some days ago, any date you like—for you know that in the theatre we manipulate time like an accordion, just as we like; the hours are drawn out and the days skimped. There's nothing easier than to have several times going at once, in all directions.

Actually, I'm afraid Madam's nerves have given way under all this strain. She isn't exactly off her head, but she has had a shock, she is *fixated,* her ideas won't change any more.

And has she succeeded in seeing her lover? Not at all. Rodrigo is under his mother's thumb now, and she is taking care of him. She's taking care of both of them.

Both, separated by thick walls, are trying to meet, rushing vainly up and down the stairs of delirium.

I am going to fetch them.

He goes out and returns with Doña Prouhèze, like a hypnotist bringing in his subject, her hand resting on his. She has put on female dress again.

THE IRREPRESSIBLE: Speak, Prouhèze! This crowd that surrounds you, though you may not know it—let them hear what you have to say! Speak, and tell us what it is that weighs on your guilty heart!

DOÑA PROUHÈZE: Rodrigo!

THE IRREPRESSIBLE: Rodrigo? He is out hunting. I mean his body is there, on the other side of those windows that glow red across the courtyard.

But in his dreams he has been trying for hours to escape from this tangled undergrowth which he hears broken and crushed in front of him beneath the weight of an invisible presence;

"Is it you?" In vain he tentatively whispers your name as you have just whispered his. There is no reply.

And soon he will come out into that glade, hoary with dead trees, clothed with immemorial moss.

There, all is strangely white against the blackness of the fir trees, even the butterfly that has spread its wings for a moment in a livid shaft of light. No one is there.

DOÑA PROUHÈZE: Rodrigo!

THE IRREPRESSIBLE, *walking backward toward the wings, without taking his eyes off* Doña Prouhèze: Come out, now, Honoria! Time to show yourself!

Enter Doña Honoria

Let this suffering creature feel her unhappy love caught up and enveloped by your mother-love,
And let your mother-heart and her lover-heart speak together.

The two women embrace.

The hour of trial approaches! I have only to set up a window frame in front of you. . . .

He signals to the stage hands who put up a window frame on which the two women lean for a moment.

. . . And you see at once what fatal fragment of Spain comes to fill it.
These mountains covered with harsh forest, matted as a bison's hair, the luminous night, the sails of the great mill on our right which interrupt the rays of the moon once every second.
And there, through the tree-shaded lanes, Don Pelagio climbs laboriously toward you, his valet going before him.

During this time the stage has been set for scene III.

Everything is in order. Come along.

He goes out leading Doña Prouhèze. Doña Honoria *remains on stage with* Don Pelagio *who has already entered.*

THIRD DAY
Scene VI
THE ACTRESS, DON RODRIGO, THE MAID

The Actress *on the apron in front of the curtain, uncorseted, with bare arms and bosom. She is supposed to be in her dressing room, getting ready for the scene she is about to play, in front of a big mirror. On her table, among her toiletries, are a few crumbled sheets of paper. All the furniture and props are attached to the curtain by clearly visible strings.*

THE LADY'S MAID, *handing the* Actress *a little pot of black stuff:* Madam has forgotten her mascara.

THE ACTRESS: You're right. A little mascara will give my eyes more sparkle. My personality is an arrow that will fly with more force from the bow of a darkened eyelid.

She touches her eyelashes with a little brush, then rolls her eyes slowly from right to left and then from left to right, opens them, shuts them, and opens and shuts them again.

THE LADY'S MAID: And all that to get an old half dead peanut seller to accept a kingdom from our hands!

THE ACTRESS: Don't say that, Mariette! You know nothing about it, Mariette. It is a superb situation! The best part I have ever had in my life! Pure gold. What a pity there's nobody to see us! But I'll use it for my season at Madrid. It'll make a little sketch at the Alcazar, you'll see!

And not a speck of rouge on the face. Only a little carmine on the lobe of each ear. What do you think?

THE LADY'S MAID, *clapping her hands:* That's enough! It lights up everything.

THE ACTRESS: Simple to begin with, expanding gradually, carefully, getting every possible shade. Quiet, gentle, smooth, with a mournful undertone. Simplicity, simplicity! A kind of resignation and submission, full of dignity. (*Trying out her voice*) La, la, la, la! Pretty butter pot! Pretty butter pot! The notes in the middle register a little veiled.

Simplicity but grandeur too! I begin with noble simplicity: "I asked you to come, Sir . . ."

She refers to the papers.

THE MAID: Does Madam wish me to fetch the script?

THE ACTRESS: There is no script, Mariette; it's much more beautiful like that. I have to create everything—words and music. I read my reply beforehand in my partner's eyes.

I only have to manage my movements nicely, and the words will come to the top by themselves.

I begin with a sort of recitation, my story, a long tissue of pathetic nonsense, recited in the most musical of voices.

And then, little by little, all the great movements of eloquence and passion, the accents of this queen, weeping at the feet of this beggar—I hope he is really hideous and brutal—and from time to time a timid word, a touching little question. That's it! here and there a delicate nothing, a spark, clear, clear, tender, touching, a sweet little *peep!*

And naturally all the time, underneath, something hidden, something feminine and secret.

THE MAID: Oh! I shall hide somewhere to watch you! Oh! if Madam is as beautiful as the other evening, it will be marvelous! I didn't know where to put myself! I cried all night!

Here the curtain rises, whisking mirror, dressing table and all, up into the air.

Good God, what's happening?

THE ACTRESS: We're on the other side of the curtain! Without noticing we've moved through to the other side of the curtain, and the action is going on without us! Oh God, somebody has stolen my part! I feel naked! Hurry, let's get back, and we'll get out of it somehow.

They go out. As the curtain rises the Actress *(another in the same part) is seen, with neck and arms bare, painting at a table, a pot of dirty water in front of her, and* Roderigo *standing over her giving instructions.*

It is interesting to note a much later comment on this play in the *Mémoires improvisés:*

None of my plays has been written with theatrical performance so clearly in mind, and you can see how I have adapted my method; there are few long speeches, and the set is continually changing so that the audience cannot possibly be bored. Consciously or unconsciously, I have come very near the technique of the Elizabethan theatre or of Calderon, or, more recently, of the cinema. This restful impression, due to variety, made it possible for the audience, to the great surprise of M. Vaudoyer, the director of the theatre, to sit, without flagging, through an act lasting two and a half hours. This is an absolutely new thing in the theatre; the audience was not tired in the slightest. This proves that I had seriously considered theatre technique, far more than in any of my earlier plays.

Part II

Experiments

The Double Actor

Sous le rempart d'Athènes is an occasional play. Claudel makes this clear in a sort of preface:[1]

When my friend Philippe Berthelot asked me to write a little play to celebrate the centenary of his father, the great scholar Marcelin Berthelot, I found myself facing a rather difficult problem. There are two methods of approach that might be considered generally suitable—the allegorical method, in which the poet has the Fatherland, Democracy, Science, and the other divinities who have been looming large in art and literature over the last few years, conversing in alexandrines; and the anecdotal method, by which we have to find a charming incident in the great man's life and turn it into a playlet with a few lyrical couplets.

Neither of these bore any fruit at all.

To speak of Berthelot is to speak of his ideas. So I decided to write a sort of philosophical dialogue or rather conversation. . . .

But Claudel seized the opportunity to make two experiments, one of them musical (Germaine Taillefer wrote the scene):

Another explanation I have to make concerns music. A play needs music. It gives an atmosphere, a continuous current that goes on after the actors have stopped speaking, and with which their words always harmonize. Its purpose is not to support and emphasize the words, but to create a sort of tapestry of sound in the background, with the play of colors to entertain and relax the audience, and pleasantly relieve the dullness of a philosophical discussion, just as the noise of a fountain or of cages filled with birds mingles agreeably with conversation. In plays or conversations, the actors must not only speak, they must listen, and they must have constantly around them something to listen to as well as something to see.

> The other experiment was more directly dramatic, and according to the report that Darius Milhaud made to Claudel, it was a complete success.

I had the idea of giving each of the characters a double, exactly like him, but nonspeaking—a kind of shadow, or perhaps *witness*, using the word not only in the legal sense but as it might be used by an engineer or physiologist. One of the figures represents that which speaks and takes part in the plot, the other simply that which is permanent, which exists, and watches us as we act. Thus each of the beautiful pillars surrounding the choir in the cathedral at Le Mans has joined to it a thin column which silently expresses the upward soaring of its slender lines.

Drama and Music

The works Claudel wrote in the years before the war were mostly commissioned, and each one gave the poet a fresh opportunity to experiment in theatrical technique.

Christophe Colomb was, as we know, the result of a commission from the producer Max Reinhardt:

I have been brooding over this project with dislike for some weeks, despite Sert's insistence. Finally, I saw Reinhardt and gave him my ideas, but without much conviction. He insisted too, and I left for Brangues. But then events took an unexpected turn. A chance remark in conversation sparked off a succession of ideas, I suddenly saw what to do, and in my enthusiasm I wrote not only the scenario as I had intended, but practically the whole play. It's as thrilling as *L'Otage* and opens up all sorts of possibilities for sets and music. I should like you to write the music for it; you would do it the way I feel it. Could you come?

This letter to Darius Milhaud was written on 2 August 1927. After this we can follow the development of the project in Claudel's correspondence with his friend and collaborator.[2] The first letter gives us the atmosphere of the play.

. . . I was thinking of you all the time I wrote this play. So you can go ahead, although I think it's a play, not an oratorio. The two things are very different. The chorus here will be inhibited at first, and the action must give an enormous kick to set it going. And we must have this dialogue between puny human voices, speaking, and the music that sometimes listens to them and sometimes drowns them. Besides, I think it may be to the advantage of the music itself to have large gaps in its fabric, without stopping altogether, while it is collecting its forces and preparing for fresh onslaughts. We should see it coming to life, and then gradually the idea should become feeling, passion.

A month later, Claudel gives fuller details about the play itself—this can be compared with what he says about the "dithyramb" when talking about *Jeanne au bûcher*—and about the music.

17 December 1927

Christopher Columbus is basically Prometheus. A man alone with all the voices of sea, sky, and nature around him. . . .

I believe we should look for a means of welding together speech and song. I have shown that everything is poetry, and that there is unbroken continuity from the lowest and coarsest words to the most sublime. The same applies to music. Everything grows from the same root, and one thing gives birth to another—feelings, noises, words, songs, cries, and music—sometimes yielding ground, sometimes claiming it. Don't you think it's a glorious idea? We mustn't have all music, and we can't have all words.

Claudel met Reinhardt and gave Darius Milhaud some details.

23 January 1928

I explained to him what you and I feel the music for this play should be like—essentially dramatic, sometimes inhibited and absorbed in its own dreams, but ever present, and from time to time sweeping all before it, then coming back to growl in its lair. What a pity I can't see you! Your ideas and mine agree perfectly on the whole. The dominant scene is that of the storm; the various effects should follow very rapidly, the whole thing short and fierce. The first based on a burst of maniacal laughter: it's coming! it's coming! it's coming! calls (not sung) and, in the middle, the piercing shriek of a madwoman, a smashed window and perhaps a cannon shot. Then the second effect, based on despairing sobs, with, above it, the shout "To the pumps! to the pumps! to the pumps!" Then silence, and the light shadows of Indians in great numbers, blown across the screen by a swift silent wind. In general, the whole play must move at a very rapid pace, and even when the music dies down, it must still be there, marking the time and escaping to make brief comments.

Scene from *La Soulier de satin* at the Comédie-Française. Production: J.-L. Barrault; sets and costumes: L. Coutaud (1943). (*Bernand*)

Scene from *Le Soulier de satin* at the Odéon Théâtre de France. New production by J.-L. Barrault; sets and costumes: Lucien Coutaud (1963). *(Bernand)*

Scene from *Le Soulier de satin* (1943). *(Bernand)*

Scene from *Le Soulier de satin* (1963). *(Bernand)*

Scene from *L'Annonce faite à Marie* at the Théâtre Hebertot. Production: Jean Vernier (1948). (*Bernand*)

Scene from *L'Annonce faite à Marie* at the Comédie-Française. Production: Julien Bertheau; sets and costumes: G. Wakhevitch (1955). *(Bernand)*

Scene from *L'Annonce faite à Marie* (1955). *(Bernand)*

Paul Claudel during rehearsals for *L'Annonce faite à Marie* at the Comédie-Française, with Denise Noël. *(Bernand)*

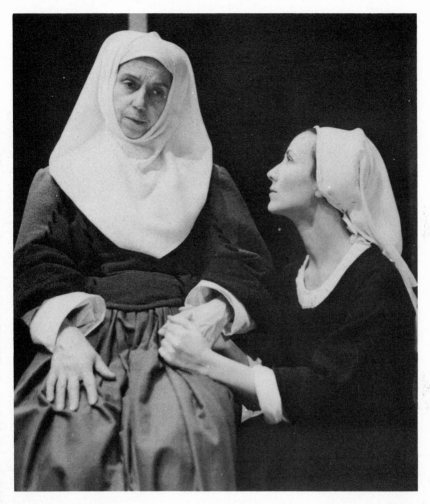

Scene from L'*Annonce faite à Marie* at the Théâtre de L'Oeuvre. Production:
Pierre Franck; sets: Pierre Simonini; costumes: M. H. Dasté (1961).
(*Bernand*)

Scene from *L'Échange* at the Théâtre Marigny. Renaud-Barrault Company.
Production: J.-L. Barrault; sets: Wakhevitch (1951). *(Bernand)*

Scene from *L'Échange* at the Théâtre de Lutèce. Production: Terzieff (1959).
(Photo Pic)

Scene from *L'Échange* at the Théâtre Récamier. Comédie de l'Est. Production: Hubert Gignoux; sets: Serge Creuz (1961). *(Bernand)*

Paul Claudel during a rehearsal of *Partage de midi* at the Théâtre Marigny (1948). *(Bernand)*

Scene from *Partage de midi* by the Renaud-Barrault Company at the Théâtre des Nations. Production: J.-L. Barrault; sets: Félix Labisse (1957). (*Bernand*)

Scenes from *Partage de midi* (1957). *(Bernand)*

Scene from *L'Otage* at the Comédie-Française. Production: H. Rollan (1950). *(Bernand)*

Scene from *L'Otage* at the Théâtre du Vieux-Colombier. Production: Bernard Jenny; sets and costumes: Pierre Simonini (1959). *(Photo Pic)*

Set by Pierre Simonini for *Le Père humilié* at the Théâtre du Vieux-Colombier. Production: Bernard Jenny assisted by Dick Sanders (1962). *(Photo Pic)*

Scene from *Le Père humilié* at the Théâtre du Vieux-Colombier. Production: Bernard Jenny assisted by Dick Sanders; sets and costumes: Pierre Simonini (1963). *(Bernand)*

Scene from *Le Père humilié* (1963). *(Bernand)*

18 May 1928

When I was thinking of my—our—*Christophe Colomb*, as I often do, I had the following idea:

After the brief shadow scene following the storm, the stage is completely blacked out. The chorus is lit only by a few candles, and only the basses are heard, beginning to croak the *De Profundis*. The stage lights are brought up gradually. The backcloth is a cold unpleasant green like that from which the black plumes of cypresses stand out in El Greco's paintings. Then a sudden *forte* as though a curtain were rising, and we see the procession emerge. A huge catafalque appears, flanked by golden statues veiled with crepe and plumed. It is escorted by masked warriors and cowled penitents carrying lighted tapers. During the whole scene, without interruption, a woman's voice, perhaps two? like a lament, or the bubbling of a stream or a madwoman. Then toward the end the character changes and the music takes on a grave tenderness while the woman's voice becomes full of love and consolation. I imagine also an instrument heard from time to time (perhaps a clarinet) which grips the heart.

The plan took shape and it was decided to put on *Le Livre de Christophe Colomb* in Berlin. Claudel deeply regretted that he could not take part in the production and insisted on one point—the use of the cinema, which he had already considered for *Protée* in 1919:

22 May 1929

I have been given the name of somebody in Berlin who specializes in the combined use of theatre and film and who is, I am told, very talented. He is called Piscator.

Piscator was not brought in, but a film was made for the production of *Christophe Colomb*. Another idea of Claudel was also put into practice:

19 January 1930

Dear Friend,

To amuse myself I drew the enclosed sketch of a possible staging for *Ch. Col.* I think the choruses (in conventional costume), who have, after all, the most essential part in the work, will have to be on the stage itself.

The action would take place on a kind of inner stage in gilded wood placed well back, which would be replaced by a screen from time to

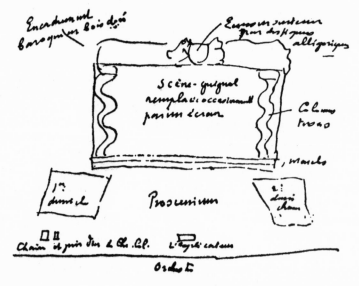

time: but there is no reason why the characters in the final scenes, for instance, should not occasionally overflow onto the apron. This arrangement would have the great advantage that we could do without sets completely, and there would be no interval between the different scenes, which is very important.

Darius Milhaud, in his Notes sans musique, gave a brief account of the production:

The setting was very clever: there was no curtain and the stage extended on both sides over the orchestra pit for the whole width of the theatre so that the chorus could sing without getting in the way of the action. At the back of the stage there was a cinema screen; film was used for greater evocative effect. When Christopher Columbus reads Marco Polo's book we see on the screen, as though in a dream, blurred outlines of exotic landscapes streaming past; during the scene in which Christopher Columbus says goodbye to his family, the same actors act the same scene on the screen but in a different setting, which doubles the action and consequently reinforces it; when Christopher Columbus questions a sailor about a wreck near the Azores, there is an enormously enlarged reproduction of the same scene which seems to extend it into a mysterious inner world.[3]

Claudel had wanted and even suggested all these devices. He wrote three pieces about the play. The first was fairly short and was written for the edition of the score:

Note on the Production of Christophe Colomb

The general idea is that the play is like a book which we open and offer the contents to the public, who, through the voice of the chorus, question those who read or act the story. They ask for explanations, join in their feelings, support them with advice and acclamation. It is like a Mass in which the congregation plays a constant part.

The audience does not only look at the actors. It wants to know what goes on in their hearts and heads, to share in the mysterious intuitions suggested to them by Fate or Providence. That is the purpose of the screen which forms the background of the stage, replacing the back-cloth. It is a spiritual landscape instead of the old material one. On it, with varying degrees of insistence and precision, all sorts of images appear, clear or blurred according to whether they exist in the present, the past, the possible, or only in dreams. Thus the play takes place half-way between the audience and a sort of visible thought of which the actors are the interpreters.[4]

He returned to one of the themes of this note in 1936, in the programme of the "concert version" given at Nantes and Paris:

The idea of the play is that Christopher Columbus is given the book of his destiny which is now accomplished, and browses through it in the presence of posterity, represented by the chorus. It is to this chorus, no less full of injustice, bad faith, flattery, and contradictions than the humanity whose resistance he once had to overcome, that he has to justify himself, now that he can read at one glance this book with his name written on the first page.

A second piece appeared in various newspapers when the play was performed:

Note on Christophe Colomb

When, a few years ago, I was commissioned to write a play about Christopher Columbus, I found myself facing a problem that cut right across the conditions of complete liberty that I ordinarily need. It was not as though I had to construct an arbitrary plot based on the discovery of America. I had myself to face this colossal fact and look at it from the point of view of posterity. I had to interpret the great store of ideas, questions, and emotions accumulated over four centuries of history. My task was to address, in the name of the whole human race, the man who united all the inhabited world. It is as though a schoolmaster put on his desk a big book containing a wonderful story, he reads it, his listeners sometimes identify with the various sentiments of the characters and sometimes reject them and demand explanations.

And, in fact, a book is brought in and placed on a desk. Someone sits before it and presents the action to the public, giving the necessary explanations. But it is not simply a reading; events are shown on the stage itself and offered for the audience to comment on.

In a word, the whole play (in about twenty episodes) is Christopher Columbus possessed by his sublime vocation, and, in the audience, now controlled, now tempestuous, now ecstatic, from the grave doubts and bitter quarrels of the beginning to the glorious jubilation of the end, a sort of anonymous murmur like the sea, the collective voice of the generations that watch and listen.

That is what I call the *chorus*. It is not the chorus of classical drama, or rather it is that same Chorus after the triumph of Christianity, when it entered the church to become the intermediary between priest and people. Between the silent crowd and the drama unfolding on the stage, a voice was needed, an officially appointed spokesman.

We see Christopher Columbus dying in the inn at Valladolid, when all the past returns before his eyes, as it moves toward its conclusion. At that moment he becomes, so to speak, his own double, spectator, and judge of his own epic story.

We see the dove, the symbol of the Holy Ghost, crossing the sea to Genoa to lay its thrilling message in the hands of a dreaming boy. We see the navigator in the Azores, at the very end of the world, hearing, in broken phrases, secrets from beyond the grave. We see the hero at grips with debtors, flatterers, and mockers. We see the captain putting down mutiny. And then comes the hour of the Passion, the opposition and criticism of little men, the hero who revealed the globe, chained to the mast of his ship and buffeted by men's rage and the fury of the elements. We see the terrible ingratitude of the whole world, except for one woman. We see the approach of death and, at last, the dove escaping as in the days of the Flood and bringing a branch plucked from this new world.

All this does not happen in a vacuum. Every voice, every word, every action brings its own echo and reply, setting up immediate or distant reactions all around. The chorus in my play has more or less the same function as the world's press, when a great event, a discovery, or a statesman's declaration gives rise to a great ferment of opinions, argument and speeches.

This conception of drama helps us to understand the part played by music. Richard Wagner's claim to glory is that he understood that every sound, from speech to song, is linked by subtle ties, and that music is inherent in everything which takes place in time; it may do no more than impose a rhythm on it, or it may gradually color it with different timbres until it opens out at last into the full glory of orchestra and chorus. Wagner's mistake was that he made no gradations between reality and pure poetry; he used the magic of a great fusion of different sounds to surround his drama immediately with a kind of narcotic atmosphere in which everything happens as in a dream. Milhaud and I, on the other hand, have tried to show how the soul gradually arrives at music, how the phrase springs from rhythm, the flame from fire, melody from speech, and poetry from the coarsest reality, and how all kinds of expression in sound, from speeches and dialogue supported by percussion and full glorious outburst of voices and orchestra, join together in one flowing torrent, diverse and yet unbroken. We have tried to show music, not only in a state of fulfillment, but *in the process of birth*, springing little by little from a deep and violent emotion.

The music of *Christophe Colomb* is infinitely varied, from the simplest to the most complex. In the same way, I realized that a fixed, immovable set would not do. We have all noticed that a fixed set, once it has made its first impact, begins to grow tiresome, and rather destroys than nourishes the poetic illusion, because it contaminates it with an inferior element. But now the producer has a new resource. Why not use the cinema? Why not consider the set simply as a frame, a foreground behind which the way lies open to dreams, memory, and imagination? When the spectator's mind is carried along on a wave of music, poetry, and action, why bring him up short against a fixed painting of a conventional landscape? Why not use the screen as a sort of projection of thought, on which all sorts of shadows and suggestions, clear or confused, flow past, mingle and separate? Why not open the doors of that cloudy world in which ideas are born of sensations? Why not use, to express the finest shades of feeling, memory, and thought, the infinitely delicate gradations of shadow? Movements, meanings, clustered shapes and shades, constantly dissolved and renewed—such is the cinema, and such, also, is music. The art and the science of shadows have reached such perfection in Germany that I should feel guilty if I did not put forward this idea to my friends who are presenting my plays in Berlin.

> Finally, when the English translation of *Le Livre de Christophe Colomb* was brought out by the Yale University Press, Claudel gave a lecture:[5]

Drama and Music

In the course of my career as a dramatist, I have often had to consider the problem of the marriage of words and music, like so many other writers from every country and every period. You all know what volumes of writing Richard Wagner devoted to the question, and one would imagine that if anyone was capable of solving it, it was this great genius, both dramatist and musician at the same time. He set himself a colossal task, and it would not be fair to say that he failed completely. *Tannhäuser* is a magnificent drama, admirably constructed, in which the music has a most poignant effect, lending depth and color to the characters' emotions. I think it is the work in which Wagner is most genuinely and completely himself. *Lohengrin* too would be a masterpiece if, like an old painting, it could be given a new canvas and stripped of all the romantic trappings which set a modern audience's teeth on edge. *Tristan* I find too uniform and monotonous, a failing shared by all Wagner's later works; and the libretto is dramatically weak. By the time a lady and gentleman have said "I love you—you love me" all through two acts, most of us have had enough; and when, in the third act, they are obviously going to start again, we are seized with utter despair, and a longing for escape against which all the clarinet solos in the world are powerless. I see now that instead of lecturing to you on drama and music, I should be giving you a lecture on love-duets. I could have vented some old grudges which, I am sure, lie dormant in your hearts as well as in mine. But I am afraid I should be carried away by my subject. However, I would like to make one observation. There are great practical difficulties in staging a love duet. During the war you must all have seen the embarrassment of artistes who had to sing some kind of national song, and thought it would make their performance look more heroic if they provided themselves with a flag. Most unwise! You can do only two things with a flag. You can wave it, or you can clasp it passionately to your bosom. There is nothing particularly startling about either of these attitudes, and when they have been struck a certain number of times, the public's emotion begins to wane. The same thing happens with love duets. The juvenile lead has only two things he can do with the prima donna—he can hold her at arm's length and contemplate her beauty with fervent tossings of the head, or he can clasp her passionately to his bosom. After a few repetitions, the audience greets these two attitudes with about as much enthusiasm as it does the ones with the flag. And at the same time as they are indulging in these gymnastics, the two singers have a much more serious task to perform: they have to do justice to a difficult and complicated score. In these circumstances their gestures are bound to lack conviction, especially when Tristan has to manipulate a somewhat generously-proportioned Isolde—as is usually the case.

To return to my subject. I am no musician, and so shall not approach it from the point of view of music and the opportunities for development which it finds in drama. I go to the opera as little as possible, and so lack experience of that kind. As far as I can see, a classical opera is a succession of items for which some sort of plot furnishes a pretext— arias, choruses, duets, ballets, overtures, trios, septets etc., all giving the musicians a chance to show off their talents. In short, it is a concert in costume, in which the orchestra fills up transitions and intervals as best it can with a vague sort of din. The difference is that in a concert the artists are allowed to stand still, whereas in an opera they think they have to indulge in conventional and ridiculous posturing completely unconnected with their essential purpose, which is to show off some long-prepared high note. And I say nothing of the costumes, sets, and production, which are uniformly lamentable, and will soon be more than the most patient audience can bear. I went to an opera called Carmen a few days ago, and I had the feeling that it might soon become difficult to get people to believe that Spaniards all wear green boleros and tight sky-blue trousers, even adorned with a pretty yellow stripe down the side.

Or if you would rather have another definition of opera, I could say that it is a dramatic plot offering a certain number of situations on which the orchestra and actors can comment in lyrical manner. For whatever a singer may do, his job is not to act but to sing. He has to express the movement of his soul with his voice rather than with his arms and legs.

Of course there is no form of art, however mediocre or absurd, that is proof against genius, or even that mysterious force, often so oddly applied, called *conviction*. That is why genius and conviction can sometimes make something of the most mediocre libretto. I could quote five or six examples of this strange happening: Gluck's *Orpheus*, Beethoven's *Fidelio*, *Les Troyens* of Berlioz, Wagner's *Tannhäuser*, Verdi's *Rigoletto*—I forget the others. However I recently had an experience which gave me food for thought. I went to a performance of Don Giovanni at the New York Opera House, and after a few moments of refreshing sleep, I realized, to my great surprise, that I was following the drama with something very like interest. And yet it is hard to imagine any form of art—or, I must confess, of music—more alien to my tastes. This mysterious force called *conviction* was acting upon me, and I was honestly sorry to have to leave before my experience was concluded.

Wagner realized the artificial and hybrid side of opera, and the painful effect on an audience of the splitting of its attention, since it cannot tell whether it is at a play or a concert. He tried to make the story more important and to keep his actors immersed in it, so that they would stop turning to face the audience. The plot is carried along on a great wave of orchestral sound, a ceaseless torrent of passion and longing, which springs from a sort of nostalgic remorseful dwelling on the past. Whereas the old operas gave the musical commentary to a tenor or a soprano, Wagner keeps it entirely for the orchestra. Suppose, for example, that the author were to express the idea: "What a lovely day! I think a walk would be pleasant." In Italian opera, the tenor would step forward with his hand on his heart, and supported by a few discreet chords, would have no difficulty in giving us his sentiments in detail. But Wagner would use the orchestra to paint a picture of the countryside, floating in a dreamlike mist of sound of which the singer's voice is a part, rising above it only occasionally and, as it were, accidentally. Wagner's drama is an immense symphony of which the real characters are the leitmotifs, and the human actors are there only to explain—generally rather laboriously—what stage we have reached, what has happened, what is happening, and what is going to happen. The human mouth opening and shutting is much less important than the silver mouth of the flute and the golden mouth of the trumpet, and it becomes lost in the constant wash of orchestral sound which this great artist loves. There is no one there—only a moving image, submerged in sound.

I certainly do not mean that Wagner had no feeling for drama. He had, and it was very deep, if not very sure. But with him every situation calls forth an earthquake of sound which engulfs everything else, and dies down a little only to rise in fresh waves very soon afterward.

I think, in short, that it would not be a bad definition to say that Wagner's dramas are symphonies with a continuous story—not an action so much as the memory of an action translated into sound.

I have said enough about the way musicians have used drama for the exercise of their art. My real purpose is to see how dramatists can use music.

There is one use which can be rejected immediately. This is when music is brought into the action as a sort of extraneous item, for example when one of the characters has to sing a little song, or a choral or instrumental item is dragged in for some reason or another. The composer is never taken into consideration, and generally he could not care less about the play, and only wants to find a home for his score. The whole plot has to be held up, with one foot in the air, so to speak, until the gentlemen with the instruments have finished making pleasant noises. What is more, there is an almost painful break between the atmosphere of pure speech and that of music, and to move from one to the other completely breaks the spell which the poor poet has taken so much trouble to put on the audience.

How is it, then, that not only the Greek theatre, but all primitive theatre up to and including the melodrama of the 1840's and the 1880's, used music?

I had my first inkling of the answer when L'Annonce faite à Marie was being produced by M. Gémier at the Comédie des Champs-Elysees. There is a scene in the play in which the father of the family, about to leave on a long journey, breaks bread for the last time with his children and servants, all seated round a table. This is one of those ideas that looks quite simple on paper, but on the stage tends to appear ridiculous; and in earlier rehearsals, I had been unable to look at this moving tableau without my spine crawling as it might at a wrong note. Gémier, with his immense experience of the theatre, did not hesitate for a minute. "We must have music!" he exclaimed. A Glockenspiel or something was brought, and the scene went off triumphantly. The music gave it the atmosphere, the environment, the dignity and distance, which speech in its arid nakedness could not provide.

Your experience of the cinema will, I am sure, suggest many similar examples to you. Mime and dumb show are simply impossible without musical support.

I took this memory with me to Japan where, as you know, I spent several years on diplomatic duties, and where I became a devotee of their admirable national drama called *Kabuki*, which is unfortunately dying out, like all beautiful things, under the influence of our crude materialistic civilization. The long hours I spent at the Imperial Theatre enthusiastically watching the heroic epics of the *Genroku* period were as good as a training school for dramatists. Unfortunately, it came a little late, at a time when I had given up my theatrical ambitions, since the modern stage is so taken up with delicate psychological debates about love that it would crumble under the heavy buskin of a hero or demigod. I understood then the meaning of dramatic music, that is, used by a dramatist and not a musician, and aimed not at painting a picture in sound, but at shocking and stimulating our feelings by variations of pitch and rhythm, more brutal and direct than speech. For example, the play is drawing to a close. The atmosphere is heavy with foreboding. Someone is coming. Something is going to happen. It is a situation which in Europe would provide work for the whole orchestra. In Japan there is simply a little yellow man perched on a platform, with a tiny cup of tea at his side, and in front of him a large drum which his job is to bang. He is the man in charge of the thunder. This single hollow sound repeated first at long intervals, then louder and oftener until the moment when the terrible apparition for which we have been waiting comes to freeze our blood, is enough, without orchestra or score, to put us in the right frame of mind. When anger mounts and two human fighting cocks are coming to grips, or when some authoritative figure is about to speak, three or four violent staccato raps with a stick on the floor of the stage are enough to impose silence. It is like a schoolmaster banging his desk with a ruler to command attention. To give another example, in *Tristan and Isolde*, when the two lovers, having drunk the fatal potion, turn, wild-eyed, to face each other, feeling in their souls the devouring passion which suddenly takes the place of hate, the tremolo of the violin, like the quiver of a breaking heart, is all the dramatist needs, and the rest of the orchestra is superfluous. Noise, rhythm, the note of a cymbal or a bell, do not give so sharp a contrast with the spoken word as music of a completely different kind. And a modern orchestra, whose path is rigidly mapped out in little black dots and bar lines on an inflexible stave is not sufficiently supple and alive. In the Japanese theatre the musician is himself an actor. He follows the play with his eyes and, at the right moment, he punctuates it freely with the help of the instrument—guitar, lyre, or even hammer—which has been put in his hand—or simply with his voice, for this is a magnificent element of Japanese theatre about which I forgot to tell you. Side by side with the articulate voice is the inarticulate voice—groans, cries, doubt, surprise, every human emotion expressed simply by the tone of voice of these official commentators squatting in their little box. When the play grips us, we are grateful to this nameless actor who cries out in our place, and expresses our feelings by something less conventional than clapping or hissing.

Music in the classical drama of Japan and China does more than express continuity. It is the *current* of the story, as we speak of the current of a river. It acts as a counterpoint to the action and maintains a long steady note beneath the vicissitudes of the story. It is there to give us the feeling of time passing, and to create an atmosphere, for in life we do not only speak and act, we listen. We are surrounded by something vague and ever-changing which we cannot ignore. If we take this view, the purpose of music is not to support and emphasize the words, but often to precede and provoke them, to stir our feelings to self-expression, to sketch a phrase and leave it to us to finish. It follows a path parallel to ours. It attends to its own business while we listen to the memories, forebodings, and advice it murmurs in our ear, and decipher our own parts. When necessary, it creates a sort of tapestry of sound in the background, with the play of colors to entertain and relax the audience, and pleasantly relieve the dullness of a description or explanation. It does for the ear what the backcloth does for the eye. In the same way, the noise of a fountain or of cages filled with birds mingles agreeably with conversation and gives a dream-like tinge to our prosaic everyday existence.

And since the meanderings of my talk have led me to China, let me tell you about a great actor who is at this moment performing in New York, and whom I was delighted to see again recently—the famous Mei Lan Fan. Mei Lan Fan plays only women or girls, but he plays them with such ethereal grace, that although he reflects them perfectly, he transcends not only all suggestions of sexuality, but even their links with the earth. What we see is neither a man nor a woman, but a sylph.

His attitudes flow from one to another so deliciously that he does not so much express every feeling and emotion as transport them into the realms of music. The music, a long recitative on the violin, with the accents marked by a drum, takes into its power the whole elegant body, from the steel spring of the legs to the smallest detail of the hands and the quick-moving fingers with their pointed nails. The music covers the whole pattern of the mime. The feet provide the spring, and the arms sketch the broad lines on which the agile fingers draw delicate traceries. The singing of this charming creature, like the humming of a flying insect, is there only to link his movements more closely with the seduction of the music, and to give the soul its part in the unfolding of the body. It is an enchanting sight, and I advise you most strongly to go and see it.

To a writer, theories are only the scaffolding, often temporary, for the work in progress. So I thought that instead of giving you dreams and doctrines, it might be more interesting for you if I showed you the work with which the ideas I have just told you about were concerned. This was commissioned, but the man for whom it was written, after a display of exaggerated enthusiasm, refused to accept it. It was all for the best, however, since my play *Christophe Colomb*, after being abandoned by M. Max Reinhardt, is soon going to be performed at the Staatsoper in Berlin, with music by Darius Milhaud. I should like to finish my lecture by telling you about this play, the first edition of which, with drawings by Jean Charlot, has just appeared here at the Yale University Press.

The specifications, if I may call them so, of the commission given me by the invisible Powers of which M. Max Reinhardt was the intermediary, opened up some interesting possibilities. A historical play was required, and all my works so far had been based on pure imagination. Music, and specifically the chorus, had to play an important part. So the whole play had to be written with a collaborator in mind, and that collaborator could be no other than my friend Darius Milhaud, whose close intellectual companionship I have enjoyed for many years. My task, then, was to look at Christopher Columbus, to browse through the pages of his history and his legend, and bring to life one by one the essential scenes. The composer, using the orchestra and choruses, would then confront me with questions, objections, and comments in the name of that public, made up of all peoples and all generations, which gathers around a great man and a great event.

A life, a vocation, the most sublime of all destinies—to discover a new world and unite all God's earth—unfolds on the stage, and the feelings and reactions aroused must naturally be expressed. With murmurs and applause, with shouts and arguments, the audience follows all the vicissitudes of the play. It is that nameless power called Public Opinion, which takes the Press as its mouthpiece, and it is also the Opinion of posterity which supports, espouses, opposes, or reinforces that of today.

In this play, then, music has quite a different role from the one it has hitherto had in the theatre. It is no longer simply a sounding board or an accompaniment to the voice, but a real actor, a composite character with many different voices blended into one. Gradually, and with mounting emotion, it sifts out from the drama itself the material of the great final hymn.

Pascal said, very aptly, "Continual eloquence becomes wearisome." I am tempted to misquote him and say: "Continual music becomes wearisome," or "Continual poetry becomes wearisome." The mind is not constantly in the same state of tension—and I am speaking now of the audience as well as the actors on the stage. It has to touch ground from time to time, if only to take off in a fresh leap. The author, and the audience with him, would do well to imitate the French wine tasters who suck a lemon from time to time to clean their mouths and enable them the better to taste the next sip of nectar. A play is not a monotonous flight against the uninterrupted purring of the orchestra. It rises and falls. I was talking a moment ago about Richard Wagner. The glory of this great man was that he understood that every sound, from speech to song, through different climates, is linked by subtle ties, and that music is inherent in everything which takes place in time; it may do no more than impose a rhythm on it, or it may gradually color it with different timbres until it opens out at last into the full glory of orchestra and chorus. His mistake was that he made no gradations between reality and pure poetry, and thus diminished his scope and impoverished his range of sound. With him, we do not penetrate gradually into a world we have conquered or earned; we are thrust without warning, by the magic of a great fusion of different sounds—particularly the brass—into a kind of narcotic atmosphere in which everything happens as in a dream. Milhaud and I, on the other hand, have tried to show how the soul gradually arrives at music, how the phrase springs from rhythm, the flame from fire, melody from speech, and poetry from the coarsest reality, and how all kinds of expression in sound, from speeches and dialogue supported by percussion to the full glorious outburst of voices and orchestra, join together in one flowing torrent, diverse and yet unbroken. We have tried to show music, not only in a state of fulfillment, but *in the process of birth*, springing and overflowing from a deep and violent emotion.

We see Christopher Columbus dying in the inn at Valladolid, where he has dragged himself in order to beg the King of Spain for the means to set out again. At that moment all his past returns before his eyes as it moves toward its conclusion, and the hero becomes, in a manner of speaking, his own double, spectator and judge of his own epic story.

We see the line of the horizon, to the West, and the dove, symbol of the Holy Ghost crossing the sea to Genoa to lay its thrilling message in the hands of a dreaming boy. We see the navigator in the Azores, at the very end of the world, hearing, in broken phrases, secrets from beyond the sea and beyond the grave. We see the genius at grips with debtors, flatterers, and mockers. We see the captain, putting down mutiny. And then comes the hour of the Passion, the opposition and criticism of little men. We see the hero who revealed the globe, chained by a cook to the mast of his ship, and buffeted by men's rage and the fury of the elements. We see the terrible ingratitude of the whole world except for one woman. We see the approach of death, and at last the dove escaping as in the days of the Flood, and bringing a branch plucked from this new world.

All this does not happen in a vacuum. Every voice, every word, every action, every event brings its own echo and reply, calling forth and spreading that anonymous murmur like the sea, which is the collective voice of the generations that watch and listen.

That is what I call the *Chorus*. It is not the chorus of classical drama, the troop of benevolent commentators and counselors, which every protagonist with sufficient power of expression appears to have been able to recruit on the shores of the Mediterranean. Or rather, it is that same Chorus after the triumph of Christianity, when it was admitted into the church to become the intermediary between priest and people. Between the silent crowd and the drama unfolding on the stage—or, if I may say so, at the altar—an officially appointed spokesman was needed.

Christophe Colomb, as it is to be given in Berlin, and perhaps one day in America, involves a new experiment which may interest you. It springs from a refusal to accept rigid partitions, either visual or aural, or to resign ourselves to a ready-made setting. We wanted our music and decor to come from within ourselves; we wanted to paint their ever-changing waves on the walls of that magic box in which we have been momentarily imprisoned. The chief characteristic of a musical play is the transformation, under the influence of time, of disjointed elements into a single melodic line—why then, should we accept a fixed set for it? Why not let the images suggested by poetry and sound be exhaled like smoke, settle for an instant on the screen, and gradually fade and give way to other dreams? In a word, why not use the cinema? We have all noticed that a fixed set, an unchanging backcloth, once it has made its first impact, begins to grow tiresome, and rather destroys than nourishes the poetic illusion, because it contaminates it with an inferior element. Then why not consider the set simply as a frame, a conventional foreground behind which the way lies open to dreams, memory, and imagination? When the spectator's mind is carried along on a wave of music, poetry, and action, why bring him up short against a fake sky as trivial and flashy as a café wall? Why, instead of all this inert matter, not offer him a surface which is sensitive to thought? Why not use the screen as a magic mirror on which sorts of shadows or suggestions, clear or confused, flow past, mingle and separate? Why not open the door to that cloudy world where ideas are born of sensations and the phantoms of the future mingle with the shadows of the past? Why not use, to express the finest shades of feeling, memory, and thought, the infinitely delicate graduations of shadow? Movements, meanings, clustered shapes and shades, constantly dissolved and renewed—such is the cinema, and such, also, is music. I believe that a marriage between these two arts is the most natural thing in the world, and that America, more than any other country, can show us how it can be done.

Opera

In November 1929 Gabriel Astruc, then director of the Théâtre Pigalle, asked Claudel to let him put on *L'Annonce faite à Marie.* Claudel at once told Darius Milhaud:[6]

22 November 1929

I have never liked the music used for *L'Annonce.* The idea is always that of a piece to be performed, which interrupts the action and ruins the effect. You remember that Mara's reading is interrupted three times. Instead of a rigidly defined piece of music, I would like the effect you get when you open an office window and hear the noise of a big town, only this time the window would be opened on to Paradise. So the first time: silence—then a confused gust of music, very short—then silence—then another gust, rather louder and immediately cut off—then silence. Mara begins reading again and we hear a vague sound from time to time as she reads.—The music comes in again. This time we hear vague, incoherent words, soft childish laughter, a rising scale of jubilation which begins, is cut off, then begins again.—Third passage of reading, with voices all the time, first weak, then becoming stronger and stronger. Mara stops reading. Then we hear a whole phrase clearly, then vague cries, immensely high, and then comes the miracle and a deep solemn bell is heard in the distance.—Would you have time to work out an impressionistic wash of sound like this? It must not be music, but a musical impression of Paradise. If you haven't time, perhaps you could give a lead to a young musician—or Germaine Taillefer? Have a word with Astruc. I should be so pleased with your collaboration. I'd like something too, for the scene of the breaking of bread, a chorale for example.

The project hung fire for a while. In May 1930 Claudel went to Berlin for a performance of *Christophe Colomb*. A few days later Astruc came to see him in Paris.

28 May 1930

I told him that in my opinion there should be a lot more music, not only where it is indicated, but in other parts too, especially in the scene of the meal and at the beginning of the second act where a background of music is really needed, something like the way we did it in *Sous le rempart d'Athènes*. I am not sure whether you really care for this idea of muffled, half-heard music, rather like the countryside breathing. If you don't like it, please tell me quite frankly. In that case, could I perhaps work with Germaine Taillefer? But, naturally, I should infinitely prefer to work with you if it isn't too unpleasant a task for you. For the last act I see an immense, gradually mounting flood of music, serving as a background and distant commentary on the verse. Is it possible??? (if necessary I could write a sort of final chorus).

The very next day he wrote Milhaud another letter:

After Astruc's visit, my imagination got to work on the music for *L'Annonce*, and I have had a few ideas which I think might be interesting; they would be a way of using your earlier discoveries.

For example, Act I, Scene iii would be built around the oriole theme:

Compère loriot
Qui mange les *cesses* et qui laisse le noyau

a clear gay little tune first played on a flute or fife, then sung by a child, then on the flute again, but already remote and drumlike, while the choir sings (p. 69, scene of the breaking of bread), then far in the distance when the father has left and the others are looking at the open door. Then the cuckoo (so mysterious and poignant) is heard three times.

A chorus based on the words of Anne Vercors (very soft and muffled) would run right through the scene, bursting into full voice only at the moment of the breaking of bread (p. 67).

"Qu'est-ce qu'il dit, le petit oiseau? Qu'est-ce qu'il dit? Qu'est-ce qu'il dit? Qu'est-ce qu'il dit? Il dit qu'il fait beau! Il dit que Dieu est grand! Midi! Il dit qu'il est Midi! Qu'est-ce qu'il dit encore? Qu'est-ce qui'il dit encore? Qu'est-ce qu'il dit encore?" (with a little shiver on *dit*, and *encore* long-drawn-out and languishing).

Since you don't like bells, and you're quite right, because they're horrible in the theatre, I have decided to cut them out completely. In Act III, page 143, when Violaine lifts her finger, all that will be heard is a woman saying:

Cloches au loin presque imperceptibles

then

Trompettes, trompettes, trompettes
Trompettes dans l'éloignement

then

Les cloches de nouveau très claires

then

Cloches au loin moins distinctes[7]

I don't think we want music for the scenes with the angels, just a sort of murmur like a crowd chanting at night, coming in gusts, with one ringing voice distinguished from the rest. The music would begin with the force of an explosion, at the very end of the third response and the third reading, jubilant but very short (perhaps something could be done with the Gloria).

And at the very end of the act, after the miracle, a joyful triumphant fanfare of trumpets.

Act IV, Scene v

"L'arrière-saison dorée"

From the third line onward, there should be a distant muffled chorus to the following words:

"O ciel! ô terre! ô lieu vraiment béni! ô sein de la Patrie!
ô terre! ô terre reconnaissante et fécondée!
"O Violaine, ô cruelle Violaine, ah quoi! désir de mon âme!
ô détestable jardin! ô amour inutile! et méconnu! Êtes-vous partie mon âme?"

And then, throughout the scene up to page 186, a long heart-rending note on the violin, becoming weaker and weaker and more and more indistinct. Then (p. 204):

"Marguerite de Paris!"

I will try to sing you the traditional tune which I feel we could use, and then (p. 207) the Angelus.

No bells! simply a woman's voice saying:

Père!
Père!
Père

and the second voice says:

Fils!
Fils!
Fils

third voice:

Dieu! ou *Pax!*
Dieu! *Pax!*
Dieu! *Pax!*

then the full peal, a chorus to the words of Marguerite de Paris, very lively and ecstatic, but unfinished.

Then on p. 208 another bell, rather shrill and rapid:

Fin!
Fin!
Fin!

then Monsanvierge, a huge, deep note:

Père!
Père!
Père!

and then the peal, full chorus, shrill and rapid:

"Marguerite de Paris—prête-moi tes souliers gris—pour aller en Paradis—qui'il fait beau! qu'il fait chaud!

rale.

j'entends le petit oiseau qui fait piiii-hihihihi-hihihih.

dimin.   *repeat with vigor*

It ends like a very shrill swallow's call with a change of key, and then Monsanvierge (the basses) says for the last time:

Père!
Père!
Père!

and then Pierre de Craon speaks the last words.

All this is only a crude outline which you may be able to do something with. Naturally I only considered it from the dramatist's point of view.

I could perhaps come and see you in a fortnight on my way to Marseilles.

With affectionate greetings,

P.C.

I am afraid you might consider these suggestions impertinent, but after all we are so used to each other and understand each other so well that we can work together and you react on me just as I do on you.

11 June 1930

For the procession of the King of Abyssinia and his wife Bellote (the two giants) (third act) I would like bagpipes and perhaps an accordion. Do you think that would be possible?

8 July 1930

I have visited the theatre, and though I think the auditorium is charming, I am not so pleased with the stage. The inner stage which is so important for my ideas will be more than thirty feet away from the audience—an enormous distance, especially as the acoustics are far from good. There are no difficulties about the choruses, nor the orchestra which could easily be placed *behind* the stage.

I have just thought that it might be a good thing to have a little music in Act III when Violaine, followed by Mara, walks through the night and the snow back to her leper's cell. There is a change of scene here, and the music could act as a connecting link.

> This score was, in fact, written and used for performances in Brussels in 1934. The information in the foregoing letters is completed by the reminiscences of Darius Milhaud (*Notes sans musique*, p. 271–272).

Claudel wanted an extensive programme of music. He came to see me at L'Enclos so that we could work out a plan. He did not want it only where the text demanded it (fanfare, liturgical chants) but also as a poetic and lyrical addition to the sound. He suggested occasional frag-

*ments of phrases repeated, leading to song, or a sung commentary,
birdsong, a long melody in praise of noonday and the delights of summer; all this would be going on parallel to the action without hindering
it. The spoken dialogue would have a kind of double, a musical shadow
drifting round it. . . . It was a reinforcement of the drama, an attempt to
do for the ear what was done for the eye in* Christophe Colomb, *when a
scene appeared on the screen showing the same action as that carried
on by the singers.*

Claudel did not stop there. His experiment with *Christophe
Colomb* led on to another project, this time unrealized and perhaps
unrealizable.

6 March 1931

I have had another idea, but a very doubtful and uncertain one about
which only you can decide, and I should welcome your opinion. It is to
make *L'Annonce* into an entirely musical drama in which music would
sometimes support the action, and sometimes disappear and then reappear. I even dream of passages in which the music would be simply
an almost imperceptible interlacing of sound waves, with the help of the
new electrical instruments which could be generally used. The chorus
of eight voices of which you speak would provide the musical axis all
the way through. No visible orchestra if possible, but a consistently
strange, supernatural, ethereal character, chanting and sobbing mingled
with the words.

I don't know if this is possible or if any theatre would be interested.
You yourself would have to take the book and carve the new play out
of it. But there are a lot of question marks.

I will make myself clearer.

Take the second act: Jacques says: *O ma fiancée à travers les branches
en fleurs, salut!* And then the chorus takes over, expressing his feelings
by means of phrases plucked from his speeches here and there.

Then Violaine says: *Jacques, bonjour Jacques!* and the chorus continues in the same way to express her sentiments, and, as the action
goes on, it constantly comments on it and reinforces it.

It is rather like the method of the Nō plays.

7 March 1931

My dear friend,

I have been obsessed by the idea I told you about in my last
letter, and I have made a rough outline of the first scene, which will

show you what L'Annonce could be like with an almost continuous background of instrumental and choral music.

Tell me frankly what you think of it?

Actually, I am very hesitant and rather inclined to say no. I can't tell what the audience will feel, continually torn between two kinds of atmosphere. It is doubtful whether the play, which was differently conceived would lend itself to it. . . . But still, you may think differently. In any case, don't be afraid of offending me by giving me your honest opinion.

Greetings,

Claudel.

If you think it worth going on, send me back the papers and the book.

8 March

I think it will be quite impossible to do.

L'Annonce faite à Marie

Three choruses.

One behind the stage (1), and in front of it a chorus of light voices (2) on the left, and one of dark voices (3) on the right.

Prologue

No. 1.

Chorus 1. "Loue ton Dieu, terre bénie, dans les larmes et l'obscurité (very clear)
        un—deux—trois—quatre (l'heure—l'heure—l'heure—l'heure)"

The barn at Combernon

Choruses 2 and 3. "Il est quatre heures du matin,
un—deux—trois—quatre   (l'heure—l'heure—l'heure—l'heure)"
not too long.

Enter Violaine. "Voici Violaine."

Enter Mara (goes to sit with the chorus, off the stage).

    "Voici Mara qui est la soeur de Violaine."

Enter Pierre de Craon. "Et voici Pierre de Craon, le bâtisseur de cathédrales."

Chorus 1 off.

ppp.

    "Loue ton Dieu, terre bénie, dans les larmes et l'obscurité!"

no. 2.
The leprosy passage (p. 10 to 14) spoken.

no. 3.
The door.
Violaine. "Eh bien, c'est moi qui ouvrirai la porte."
Violaine, Jacques
"J'ai ouvert la porte."
and the three choruses
"Elle a ouvert la porte."
at the same time

no. 4.
The bell (chorus 1).   RE
GI
NA
Violaine.   *Regina coeli laetare Alleluia.*
Chorus 2.   *Regina coeli laetare Alleluia.*
Chorus 3.   *Regina coeli laetare Alleluia.*
The bell (ch. 1)   MA
RI
A
Pierre de Craon.   *Quia quem meruisti portare Alleluia.*
Chorus 3.   *Quia quem meruisti portare Alleluia.*
Chorus 2.   *Quia quem meruisti portare Alleluia.*
The bell (ch. 1)   LAE
TA
RE
Violaine.   *Resurrexit sicut dixit Alleluia!*
Chorus 2.   *Resurrexit sicut dixit Alleluia!*
Chorus 3.   *Resurrexit Alleluia!*
Chorus 2, 1.   *Gaude et laetare Virgo Maria Alleluia!*
Chorus 3, 2.   *Quia resurrexit Dominus vere Alleluia!*
Silence.
The bell (ch. 1).   *Laetare Laetare Laetare Laetare Laetare* etc.
    Lae ta re   Lae ta re
    Lae   ta   re
Choruses 2 and 3 together
with the two actors.   Latin prayer on page 17.
A voice off
"Loue ton Dieu terre bénie dans les larmes et la félicité!"

no. 5

Pax tibi (intoned).

Pierre de Craon.

Pax tibi

page 18, where marked in pencil.

The following lines are divided antiphonally, like a psalm, between the two choruses

The penultimate line twice repeated

What follows (Violaine) recited or intoned:

Chorus 2. "Quand déjà au travers des murs diaphunes de tous côtés."

Ch. 3. "apparaît le sombre paradis."

Ch. 2. "Et que les encensoirs de la nuit se mêlent à l'odeur de la mèche infecte qui s'éteint."

Ch. 1. "Loue ton Dieu, terre bénie, dans les larmes et la félicité."

no. 6.

P. Quel est l'anneau d'or, Violaine, que vous portez au doigt?

V. Un anneau que Jacques m'a donné.

P. Je vous félicite.

V. Ce n'est, etc.

Prenez mon bel anneau et donnez-le à ma soeur Justice!

Sainte Justice de Reims que vous nous avez racontée. De quoi vous êtes architecte.

P. Que dira votre fiancé?

V. Ce n'est pas encore mon fiancé tout à fait.

P. J'accepte cet or pur.

then p. 24 and 25.

The dialogue becomes more and more animated, and Violaine's speech "Loué soit Dieu . . ." becomes a jubilant song with choruses 2 and 3 joining in, as far as ". . . reconnaissable au loin."

Chorus 1. "Reconnaissable au loin."

no. 7. The lark.

Chorus 2. "Ah! que ce monde est beau et que je suis heureux."

V. "Ah que ce monde," etc.

Follow the pencil underlinings.

"C'est l'alouette! C'est l'alouette! hi! hi! hi! hi! hi! can be sung. Waves?"

no. 8.

P. "J'emprunte l'anneau."

V. underlined
P's speech can be partly sung, supported by chorus 3.

no. 9. The farewell.
underlined
1. ". . . Mais celle que je vais faire sera sous sa propre ombre."
2. "Comme de l'or condensé."
1. "Mais celle que je vais faire sera sous sa propre ombre."
2. "Elle sera sous sa propre ombre comme de l'or condensé, comme une pyxide pleine de manne."

no. 10. The farewell.
underlined
She takes him by the shoulders. They gaze at each other for a long time.
Chorus 1. "L'heure. L'heure. L'heure. L'heure. L'heure.
    Adieu Violaine, mon âme, je ne vous verrai plus."
Ch. 2 and 3. "Adieu! Adieu! Adieu!
    Adieu Violaine, mon âme, je ne vous verrai plus."
The kiss.
Ch. 1. "Adieu, Violaine, mon âme, je ne vous verrai plus!"
Ch. 2 and 3. "Loue ton Dieu, terre bénie, dans les larmes et la félicité."

> They had to keep to the original plan, and Claudel gave some final advice—to no purpose, as it happened, because the Théâtre Pigalle abandoned the production.

W., 31 October 31

My dear friend,

I have received the letter you wrote after your interview with Fouilloux. I can't say I'm very enthusiastic about the idea of canned music throughout. Quite the opposite in fact. I am afraid the result will be something completely dead and artificial, which is diametrically opposed to what I was looking for. I want music that appears to emanate from the words rather than accompany them, passing imperceptibly from the realm of feeling to that of sound. And what are we going to do about the boisterous march of the peasants in the third act and the funeral march in the last? However, it's you, after all, who are mainly concerned, and if you are satisfied I can't refuse to give it my blessing—reluctantly, I admit.

I have no preferences as to the date of performance.

For some scenes I would like to duplicate the characters as in *Sous le rempart d'Athènes.* Would Fouilloux mind? He could make it up on the sets which I want as simple and even rudimentary as possible. If he likes, I'll send him a detailed plan.

I feel that we need a little music at the end of the prologue, for example

1. Vague noises, then

2. *Laetare, laetare, laetare, laetare, laetare, lae-ta-re* (very rapid, diminuendo and rallentando, then)

3. Lae-
      -ta
Silence
Greetings,

P. C.

The effect of the canned music for *Donogoo* was lamentable.

It will be very difficult to fit all that mechanical stuff into live dialogue.

Japanese Nō Drama

Le Festin de la sagesse is Claudel's own title and very little explanation is needed. *Le Festin de la sagesse* was commissioned by Ida Rubinstein in 1934. The music was composed by Darius Milhaud. But the work was not as successful as *Jeanne au bûcher* or even as *Christophe Colomb*.

Claudel's commentary on it appeared in the *Revue de Paris* in July 1938, but the manuscript seems to have been written at the same time as the mime play.

Thanks to the work of Arthur Waley, Noel Péri, and especially Colonel Renondeau, the European public is becoming better acquainted with the very specialized technique of the Japanese Nō drama, which is in my opinion one of the highest forms of lyrical and dramatic art achieved in any country. I myself have analyzed its spirit and characteristics in my book *L'Oiseau noir*. But in the same way as Lord Kelvin said he could not understand a theory of mechanics until he saw it working in the form of a machine, an engineer of the imagination, faced with a new form of his art, is always irresistibly tempted to take a hand and *see what happens* if he uses it to work out whatever theme his good or evil genius may suggest to him. That is what I have tried to do, with the kind collaboration of Mme. Ida Rubinstein, in a version of the Nō drama that will be presented to the public in a few months through her good offices. The subject is the well-known parable of the Feast, taken from the Gospels.

The Nō plays, almost two hundred and fifty in number, all date from the feudal period, that of the Fujiwara shoguns, and so are contemporary with early Kano art. They are deeply religious and national in character. It is an essentially aristocratic art, intended for the entertainment of a small group of cultured amateurs. Even today the performance of these plays, which can only be compared with the Spanish *autos*, tends to be esoteric. The actors have the solemnity and reverence of mystics, while the audience brings a disciplined attention, and a mind sharpened and purified by abstinence from every outside distraction, which is a rare state and difficult to achieve, but necessary for the appreciation of a great work of art as for the highest spiritual teaching. The main parts are assigned to specialists belonging to families who have maintained for centuries the traditions of four schools, and who prepare for their work by a twenty-four hour period of meditation. The minor parts, and those of singers and instrumentalists, are taken by distinguished men who, in the same way, undergo a long preparation. In one of the plays I attended, the "shoulder drum" was played by a civil engineer. The audience is pitiless, expecting from the actors the most minute attention to detail and complete absorption in the character. In one of the most remarkable plays I have seen, *The Bell*, the priest being slowly and inexorably attacked by a vampire has to remain motionless for almost an hour without even blinking, and a knowledgeable and merciless audience is there to see that this appearance of petrifaction is maintained. I have told elsewhere the story of the daimyo who ordered one of his henchmen to watch a famous actor and kill him at once if he saw the slightest sign that his attention was wandering. The play went through without a hitch. But the swordsman said in answer to questions,

"The actor hesitated a moment and I already had my saber raised, then the flow of his thoughts went on as before."

"That is true," said the actor. "I caught sight of a speck of dust on the polished platform, and it disturbed me for a second."

The subject of these little plays, which are divided into two parts, is basically always the same. A supernatural being meets and talks with a witness, a priest, warrior, man or woman, planted there like a human pole. The masked figure, engulfed in brocade of incredible splendor, walks with such solemn, majestic tread through the long corridor and onto the stage, which, shaded by a canopy, gleams like an unsubstantial surface. Each of these steps, by turns lingering and firm, like the divisions of a train of abstract thought, each of these delicately balanced attitudes, alternately broken and renewed, suggests the crossing of unbelievable distances from one world to another. And, meanwhile, the newcomer and the Chorus describe the journey in a long antiphonal poem. Then comes the often poignant exchange of question and answer, whose bitter conclusion is always the vanity of human joy and sorrow, and it all ends in a ritual mime, unless the Apparition reenacts the mystery of its birth by a hypnotic withdrawal.

I would like to lay special stress on two characteristics of Nō drama which strike the European spectator. I shall not touch the literary and musical study of the texts (which is very interesting). It has been done by the excellent scholars whose names I have given above.

The first of my notes concerns the use of the Chorus. The Japanese dramatists realized that the great human issues, the typical confrontations of thought and feeling, do not develop only between two people linked vaguely by events or words, even though they may be of graver import than our usual feeble chatter. The Word is creative. Every word man's lips utter, every truth he expresses, causes a series of echoes, replies, memories, appeals, and contradictions in vast concentric circles, opening around it like a flower. A circumstance is modified by an idea, a sound can shake a soul, and a sentence uttered at one moment in time has its repercussions at great distances. The Chorus in Nō drama (and I mean the chorus of instruments, or orchestra, as well as that of voices) has a double role. First of all it is the listener. It takes a word from the lips of the actor and weaves it into a tapestry of images and sayings. It adapts thought to speech. But both above and below poetry and music, Nō drama adds a third element, which is the exclamation, the cry, the reverberation of the character's emotion until it returns to him again. That is what is called in Japan the *Ah!* Laughter, sobs, grumbling, protestation, invective and the lash of the whip—all the reactions of a sensibility directly assaulted.

A second characteristic of Nō drama which we find remarkable is the slowness of the gesture. Important things are happening between the representative of the other world and that of human life, motionless at the foot of that post which is for him a tree. That phantom did not escape from Eternity and seek out a witness merely to assail him with empty prattle and silly gestures. Every movement has its meaning, its own part in the message. To the watcher, each one is an event, a manifestation of fate. The gesture begins with the breathing and the movement of the shoulder, and by the time it has passed through every joint of the arm and hand to reach its termination, the onlooker's eye and mind has been able to follow and understand this message of another's will to ours, this unfolding of a thought to the very tips of the fingers. In the same way, the steady advance of a human being, shifting his weight from one leg to the other, has such terrible majesty and fateful solemnity that even a foreigner cannot help but feel the crawling of gooseflesh under his skin. This is more than simply an artist's imagination, and the poet did not draw his characters from mere random fancy. These islands, where the ground is ceaselessly shaken by warning tremors, are not called the land of the Kami for nothing. There had to be a priest-magician, still very near to the mysteries of Polynesia, to pluck these dark flamboyant figures from the book of nightmare.

The third remarkable point in the technique of these sacred plays is the costume. When the curtain rises, we see the stage, an emptiness quite apart from space and time as we know them, a place for entirely imaginary action, and thence, whether we like it or not, symbolic. The audience, then, vaguely expect something more "contrived" than the reflections of themselves they see in the windows of dress shops. In both speech and dress, they need something belonging exclusively to a world of ideas. In answer to this demand, the producer has first to divest his actors firmly of the common uniform of drawing room and street; he has then three possible solutions. The first is impersonality. This is the classical solution—the peplum, covering the body, as the verse speech covers the emotions, with its abstract folds. The second is the recourse to history, with its castoffs all ready to be dragged out of storage. The third solution, infinitely more difficult and dangerous, is the recourse to symbolism. We have an example in the dress of priests performing a ritual act. The liturgical meaning of, for example, the cope, the maniple, and the miter, has often been explained, and so, in another domain, have the regalia of freemasonry. In the same way, in Nō drama, the Warrior, the Old Man, the Priest, the Hermit, the Wife, the Widow, the Virgin, the Serving-maid, the Grandmother, are confirmed in their roles by mask and headdress. They wear their costumes like a kind of aura around them, like the two pairs of dazzling wings that nature has attached to the back of the butterfly. The huge fullness of the robe, the cloak, and the sleeves, the headdress with its brilliant decorations, the scarlet or inky-black mane adorning gods and demons, all give the apparition that lyrical quality which we find at Bayreuth, rising from the darkness beneath the feet of Wotan and Loge. And since I was speaking of wings a moment ago, I cannot leave out the ethereal fluttering of the Fan which, in the hands of the actor, is like a message plucked out of the air, as though he were offering us his own breath.

When Mme. Ida Rubinstein asked me to write a biblical piece, with music by my old friend and faithful collaborator Darius Milhaud, I quite naturally turned my thoughts toward the sacred drama of Japan, which I had watched assiduously and admiringly for five years.

As it happened, I had among my notes a plan for a sort of dramatic oratorio, the subject of which was taken from the famous parable of the Feast as told by St. Matthew and St. Luke. A king prepares a great feast for his son's wedding and sends his servants in all directions to fetch the guests. But each of them has an excuse for staying away. One is getting married, another is trying out a yoke of oxen. The servants return empty-handed. But then the king sends them, armed with whips, into the highways and public places to bring in all comers. *Compel them to come in!* And there they stand in the king's hall, men and women, and each wears a wedding garment. Only one appears insufficiently dressed, and he is shamefully cast into outer darkness where there is *weeping and gnashing of teeth.*

(I admit to having been particularly interested in this solitary delinquent, and I was very sorry to have to leave him out. In one of my first sketches, inspired by American cartoons, I had him dressed simply in a barrel, without a bottom, hung over his shoulders by straps. He was doing a mad Pyrrhic dance, while the screams of Pandemonium offstage mingled with the triumphal chant of the Elect. But I had to maintain decorum, and I dared not introduce into the action one of those discordant elements for which, as I realize with regret, the public does not share my taste.)

I also had to find a part suitable for my leading actress.

It was then that I remembered the books of Solomon or his Alexandrine imitators which I have studied with such interest and devotion all my life—Proverbs, Ecclesiastes, Wisdom, and Ecclesiasticus. They have a female character in whom the Fathers of the Church have seen a prefiguration of the Virgin and of the Church itself. This is Wisdom, who, in Chapter VIII of Proverbs, is shown as entrusted with the very mission described in the Gospel—the calling of the prodigal and recalcitrant to the communion of God. Elsewhere she is compared with an honored mother, and Solomon weaves in her honor a garland of enchanting comparisons which the Church only needs to borrow to add fresh incense to its liturgies.

But actually the Books of Wisdom are not the only ones to reflect the Palm of Kadesh and the Rose of Jericho. And at every point in the Gospels where the Virgin appears, the exegetist feels in his heart the dew distilled at the approach, through human passions and through the desert of time, of Her who is called Grace and also Wisdom. Wisdom is a truth known not only to our intelligence as an abstract theory, but to our whole being as a fact; not only to our mind, but to our soul, to our complete self, to that deep understanding which contains within it all the knowledge and all the needs of our physical and moral nature.

That is how I found the religious theme, which comes not from legend or superstition, but from one of the most essential episodes of the great drama of our redemption. It fell of its own accord into four movements or acts.

In the first, Wisdom, who according to the Book of Proverbs was *set up from the beginning*, and, before the creation of the world, when God *set a compass upon the face of the depth*, and *gave to the sea his decree that the waters should not pass his commandment*, was *daily in his delight, rejoicing always before him*, appears before the Lord to ask permission to go in search of erring man, that eternal Prodigal Son. She receives, together with the authority, the distinctive sign of her mission upon her shoulders.

The second act shows us Wisdom seeking her guests. At first I had thought of setting it in a sort of theatre, with boxes on both sides, each box occupied by a group representing a human activity: for example, a studio, a family meal, a laboratory, a den of thieves, a gaming-house, a hospital, a boxing match, a school lesson, a mine, a ship in a storm. Behind these boxes Wisdom would have been seen in procession, preceded by a cross, while the Chorus sang the anthem: *Venite ad nuptias.* I ended by preferring a simpler idea.

The third act is the illustration of the terrible proclamation of the Gospel following on the intimations of conscience: *Compel them to come in!* The whip is placed in the hands of the nimble auxiliaries of Love. Disease is a whip, war is a whip, poverty is a whip, woman is a whip. The ferret is set in the rabbit warren of mankind.

And the fourth act shows us Wisdom at her table amid the plans for the palace she is building, of which seven pillars are already standing. The workmen, dressed in the wedding garments which are none other than their working clothes, come to claim the wages she has promised them, for it is noon, when the sun stands high, and they are hungry. They take their places at the table, and Wisdom herself sits on her radiant throne above them all. The servants bring forth all the meats and the fruits of earth and water, and the Pascal Lamb in the midst. Then the eight acclamations of the Gospel ring out: *Blessed are the poor in spirit! Blessed are the meek! Blessed are the peacemakers! Blessed are the pure in heart! Blessed are they which do hunger and thirst after righteousness! . . .* And the play ends with the Hymn of the Apocalypse: *Holy, holy, holy, Lord God Almighty, which was, and is, and is to come. . . . Worthy is the Lamb to receive power, and riches, and wisdom, and strength, and honor, and glory, and blessing, for ever and ever, world without end! Amen!*

The theme I have just outlined gave me the chance to continue studying a facet of the theatre which my work up to this point has led me to consider of the utmost importance. We still find actors—and very rare they are—for whom language is more than a means of expressing one's thoughts and feelings in an easy-going, slapdash sort of way. They study their lines with the same careful ear, the same intricate preparation as the musician brings to his score. But as for gesture, no modern actor ever appears to attach the slightest importance to it. Anything will do. Most of the time, speech is accompanied by a brief nervous movement of the forearm and a kind of tremolo of the hands, varying in rapidity according to the emotion which the character is supposed to be feeling. Not one of them has the slightest idea of the immense variety of means of self-expression which the human body—I mean the whole human body, from the head and face to the toes—can bring to drama. (I say drama and not beauty, because I am one of those who believe that the purpose of art is not beauty, but the expression of feeling. Beauty is a by-product only obtained when you are not thinking about it.) In my recent work for the production of the *Choephori* in Brussels, I tried to fit a whole lyrical speech with the movement of the arms slowly lifting an amphora then crashing it down, and it made a considerable impression. Anyone can see the difference between the gesture of a man who knows what he is doing, and that of a madman stammering with all his limbs. Let us take the simplest and most banal of gestures, which, in popular illustrations, expresses the despair of the level-crossing attendant seeing her child in danger from a train—a hand brought up to the face. It is quite uninteresting. But do it very slowly, as an actor in a Nō play would, and the emotion is intense; you are lifting a weight, bringing a terrible letter close to your eyes, gazing into a mirror. We see a being becoming conscious, with mounting horror, of his own identity, staring at his hand and knowing the momentary blindness it is about to bring him. We see Fate itself, and know in our hearts that it is our own. In very swift gestures too—those which throw the whole body into a sort of flashing arabesque, like picking up and throwing a stone, cracking a whip or gathering oneself for flight—nothing must be left to chance. It is a superb art, almost forgotten today, which ought to be studied. Painters and sculptors cannot help us much. The most remarkable thing about the art of every age is the insipid and conventional nature of the gestures and attitudes conceived entirely as part of a fixed composition. The dramatist is interested in the intense, utterly significant expression, the lightning flash of truth with which the body responds to a given situation; but this is almost entirely lacking in the world of oil and stone, in which death has the ascendancy over life. Italian art is especially deficient in this way, as it was easy to see it at the recent exhibition.

There only remain costumes and sets, and the reader who has followed me as far as this will easily guess where my preferences lie. French taste is definitely in favor of whatever is consistent and logical, and we tend therefore to see a dramatic production not as a random juxtaposition of all branches of art—sound, speech, movement, and color—but as a *creation* in which the idea, once started, both gives to and takes from art what each needs to express itself. To return to the scenario I was just outlining, Wisdom is not merely accomplishing her mission in a more or less decorative disguise and a pictorial setting which the author is kindly offering her. She has created it all—her costume, her supporting actors, the stage itself. The lines are spoken, and replies and explanations come from all sides; the voice calls up the Chorus. Wisdom appears, and everything around her exists to give her expression and to endow with solidarity and shape the furrow she traces in the realities of life. Such is the set for the first act, which is basically a screen of mountains like crossed curtains, brought to audience level by the sea with its regular tiers of waves prolonged by a cataract of steps, while two twisted columns, with their double movement like muscles, up and down, unify all planes, directions, and dimensions.

But the essential theme of the visual side of this production is the Road. In the form of a long stole covered with Greek letters, like the phylacteries of the Scriptures, it lies on Wisdom's shoulders as the sign of her ordination. The watch over distant horizons is the reason for her tall headdress, like an observation tower. The Road, personified and carried along by Distance, rolls and unrolls the miles and leagues around an invisible reel, and takes the band of Travelers farther and farther away, from one horizon to another. The long, long lines of the Road, black and gold by turns, like the scrawled writing in an enchanter's book, clothes the Ambassador of the Almighty and winds its endless spirals around the bodies of her Servants. And in the last act the Road is halted in its flight, and a piece is cut off to become a table to which all the fruits in Creation are brought for the Universal Communion, for the prodigious Feast of Wisdom and her guests, in the sight of God.

A Dithyramb

At about the same time as Ida Rubinstein commissioned *Le Festin de la sagesse*, for which Darius Milhaud was to write the music, she commissioned a play on Joan of Arc, with a score by Arthur Honegger.

The circumstances in which *Jeanne d'Arc au bûcher* was conceived and the problems it posed were explained in a lecture which Claudel gave several times, on the occasion of performances in Switzerland, Belgium, and France. We have taken from it the two following passages:[8]

Historical Drama

Contrary to what is generally thought, it is difficult to write an imaginative work about a great historical figure. The author does not have the freedom he needs, and cannot construct his work as he wishes. All he can do is to color a drawing that has already been made. The character to whom the poet is trying to give life, speech, and movement is not entirely the child of his own thought. My essential task is not here to weave a representative plot through which I can interpret the feelings, passions, and struggle of a being who develops as he encounters various obstacles, among voices calculated to chime with his own. The hero taken from history follows a course laid down beforehand; he escapes on all sides from the artificial, closed environment which constitutes a work of art, that logical, compact situation in which the demands of the story take the place of outside influences. That is why a poet—for example Corneille or Racine—generally tries to strip a character of his historical attributes. All he leaves him is a name, something decorative like a plume or an escutcheon, under cover of which Titus or Nero acts and speaks according to the demands of the mainspring of classical theatre, which is gallantry.

But it can also happen that the historical character chosen by the poet is too colossal a figure to be conjured with. He has disappeared in his own legend. He appears before a public who, so to speak, already knows him by heart, and demands from him certain fixed speeches which seem to have been his sole justification for appearing at all. For instance, if General Cambronne appeared in a play about the army, he would not be tolerated without the heroic exclamaion which legend attributes to him. Figures like Napoleon or Jesus Christ are not puppets whose strings can be pulled at will. As soon as they appear, the poor author can only go with them, hat in hand, and make sure that everything is in order so that they can utter the historic words for which the audience is patiently waiting. Everything happens in perfect sequence, like a Church service. It is a sort of ceremony, instructive, profitable and edifying, but not very enjoyable for anyone, least of all for the author.

The difficulty is especially great for Joan of Arc. There is certainly no more marvelous and touching story in the world, nor one which seems at first sight more perfectly suited to the stage. But there is also no story better known and leaving less free play to the author's imagination. We cannot do what we like with Joan of Arc; in fact, it is she who does as she likes with us, and simply by being there restricts us to the inglorious role of bystander or impresario. We cannot make Joan speak, we can only let her speak; and the way she spoke has come down to us inescapably in the authentic reports of her two great trials. It has been said that we cannot "gild refined gold nor paint the lily." The saying applies perfectly to the words of Joan of Arc.

So when Arthur Honegger came to ask me to write the scenario of a play on Joan of Arc for which Mme. Ida Rubinstein had commissioned him to write the music, I received him without the slightest enthusiasm. I detailed to him all the arguments I have just given you, and he went away disappointed. Immediately afterward I had to take a train to Brussels. I had just finished skimming through some evening paper or other and was about to go to sleep in my corner when, clear and startling as an electric shock, a gesture took shape before the half-closed eyelids of my mind.

The Creative Power of a Gesture

All artists know that instant of conception when the idea of a new work comes like a wasp to alight on our consciousness and sting that creative power which is always there, dormant in our soul—and dare I say in our body too?—to a state of half-awakeness. Sometimes it is a word, sometimes a memory, sometimes a feeling, or even less than that, a kind of dark impulse from the time before sound ever was. This time it was a gesture which I saw performed over and over before my eyes, appealing to wider and wider areas of longing and imagination, composing around itself one scene after another. And the gesture held for me all the more meaning because Arthur Honegger had been talking to me about the undisputed mistress of movement and attitude in the world today, Mme. Ida Rubinstein—and this artist was asking me to write a play about Joan of Arc.

This gesture was the sign of the Cross

The sign of the Cross is when the hand starts from the hollow of the chest, rises to the forehead, comes down again to the heart, moves left and right to touch on each shoulder the source of our physical actions, and in a cycle which confirms our creation and affirms our salvation, takes in the four cardinal points of the human entity. What better starting point could there be for a mime play in which the body is summoned by a high ideal to make use of every means of expression it possesses?

But I saw this sublime gesture performed before me, not merely by one careless hand, but with pain and difficulty by the two hands of a young girl, bound together with an iron ring. This gave me my subject. It evoked and sanctified the whole play. Just as Christ cannot be separated from his cross, so Joan of Arc must not be separated from the instrument of her passion, her martyrdom and her sanctification—the stake. *Jeanne d'Arc au bûcher.* That must be the span of this work which was imposed upon me by the coincidence of an external circumstance and an inner revelation. I felt in the air a behest which I dared not refuse.

They say that the dying, in the minute before the end, see in a flash the image of all the events of their past life. In the same way, we may suppose that for Joan of Arc, as for her divine model, the words "And I, if I be lifted up from the earth, will draw all men unto me" have become reality. Joan of Arc, too, is "lifted up," and from the height of her fire like Christ from the height of his cross, she draws everyone to her. She can measure at a glance the way she has come, and unite all its stages into one. She can see fully realized her sublime vocation, supremely borne on the flames beneath her feet. From Rouen to Domrémy, she traces back her steps, and this consummation gives them their meaning. For this obedient daughter, now that God is at her side to see her completed task and tell her the secret of his purpose, the time has come to understand what she has done.

The Music

In order to render the passion and ascension of Joan of Arc intelligible to a modern audience again, I felt that words were not enough. It needed something fuller and more lyrical to give it strength and force. The *voices* that sound beneath the surface of history must be heard, and that is why music is indispensable. It intensifies the rhythm, opens the heart, in the same way as the chord spreads, to every passion, impregnates speech with feeling and thought, and both speaks and listens at the same time. A great musician, M. Arthur Honegger, has consented to write the music. As for Joan herself, I have not tried to show either the little peasant girl or the heroine of history, but the saint, with her aureole already about her. I have tried to expand and amplify that moment which, we are told, comes before every death, when it is granted to every actor in the drama of human life to see and understand the part he has played. We may even think that the sovereign Father, before admitting her to the place where all tears are dried, allows her, from the height of the sacrificial fire and in the light of the flames that consume her, to read page by page, backward, the whole history of her life, from Rouen to Domrémy. And thus completely aware of the mission entrusted to her, with a cry that mounts like a flame, she utters her last glorious *yes*.

> In a later text, dated 4 January 1951, Claudel harks back to the classical form of drama known as the "dithyramb."

I have always been attracted by the primitive form of drama called *dithyramb*, of which the *Suppliants* of Aeschylus is the only surviving example. One solitary figure, the only one with a face of his own, speaks amid a semicircle of voices which, simply by being there, lure and compel him to speech. Every poet has known this auditory horizon, this confused murmur of jumbled phrases, echoing and reechoing until at last they give birth to words. The Greek Chorus later gave it a liturgical form which has been perpetuated in Church services. So when Mme. Ida Rubinstein asked me to make Joan of Arc the subject of a dramatic poem supported by vocal and instrumental music, I naturally thought at once of a kind of Mass. This too was a solemn sacrifice, the redemption by an innocent being of a people crushed beneath a worse evil than oppression—the lack of certainty.

Schopenhauer, misunderstood by Wagner, said with great profundity that music is the expression of Will in search of a form—or, one could say, a reply. To let ourselves be carried away by the dark upsurge of elemental forces is no reply. We are all aware of the painful clash between the spheres of song and speech. Honegger and I have tried to derive an element of drama, and thus of emotion, from that very clash.

Joan is tied to her stake, which represents Faith. She is rooted in an unshakable certainty, and is one with it. Around her, tier upon tier in the darkness, are the people to whom she has been thrown as their representative and their sacrifice, as, in the Roman amphitheatre, virgins were thrown to the lions. And in the first scene of the play, Joan is in fact thrown to the lions.

But little by little she gains the upper hand. Her voice, charged with meaning, replies to a more and more attentive ear. Her hearers are trying to understand. Everything she has undertaken and accomplished in obedience to a call from above—"Go, daughter of God!"—the banner held in her left hand and the sword brandished in her right, all this she explains and recreates in triumph! And little by little the atmosphere changes. Doubt, insults, shouts of incomprehension and hate, give way to faith and enthusiasm. "Joy is the strongest, Hope is the strongest, Love is the strongest." The fire springs up on all sides as in the Hymn of St. Francis. Praise be to our sister Fire, for she is pure, strong, living, active, eloquent, invincible, indivisible, until Joan raises to heaven her bound hands and the chains fall away. . . .

God is the strongest.

And the play ends with these words, three times repeated with ever-deepening solemnity.

Greater love hath no man than this, that a man lay down his life for his friends.

Poems in Movement

This work was not published till late, but it is dated 26 January 1938, and was thus written shortly before *L'Histoire de Tobie et de Sara*. It probably marks the farthest point reached by Claudel in his research into the realm of gesture.

A few scattered allusions in a letter to Darius Milhaud, dated 14 November 1937, appear to refer to it. It is not even a mime play, but a few simple gestures linked by dialogue. They are listed at the beginning of the scenario:

Programme of Movements

1. The conquest of the right hand by the left.
2. The awakening.
3. Reflection in the fountain.
4. The arrow.
5. The flung stone.
6. The rose.
7. The bunch of grapes.
8. The sower.
9. Rain.
10. Destiny.
11. Apollo and Daphne.
12. The sign of the cross.

No writings of Claudel on these "poems in movement" are known. The project was very soon abandoned. The aim seems to have been to give these movements all their aesthetic value by performing them very slowly, as in Nō drama.

ALIKI: A stone in the grass, a stone on the ground, a stone I did not see, like an epitaph—here!

She picks up from the ground and examines carefully something which we take to be a piece of stone.

NADA: What name is on it? What writing?

ALIKI: No name, but I recognize it. It is the stone of Destiny on which our foot suddenly stumbles.

Ah yes, and we are told we must learn to direct our gaze, as though in a mirror.

She begins a gesture.

NADA: No—you move too quickly. What you are to show is the most banal gesture of all, the fear and horror of the crossing attendant in the illustrated papers, who puts her hand to her face when she sees her son caught by the train! The whole thing is to move slowly, slowly, and very carefully! Like someone lifting a weight! or a mirror! Or like someone bringing a sentence of death close to his eyes, to study it and offer it as food to his terror-stricken soul.

A Parable

The last work written during this period, *L'Histoire de Tobie et de Sara*, is interesting from many points of view. It was again commissioned by Ida Rubinstein, who dreamed this time of a collaboration between Claudel and Stravinsky. It uses all the resources of music, choreography and the cinema. Talking about this play, Claudel returns yet again to the idea that a play is a parable. It also marks the return to a more directly dramatic conception of the theatre.

L'Histoire de Tobie et de Sara consists of three acts, about seventy pages, enough to fill a whole evening. In one or two weeks, I shall have finished copying it. The spoken, purely dramatic part is very important. There is a septet of the Trees of Paradise with the chorus at the end of the second act and at the end of each act a long mime sequence (I don't know quite what to call it) for Ida.[9]

Claudel discusses music in two letters to Milhaud.[10]

15 August 1938

Once more we shall have to discuss this thorny question of music *in the process of birth* and music springing from poetry as poetry from prose, and prose from silence and the formless mutterings of the mind. It is very difficult, and we shall have to reach perfect understanding on the subject.

5 September 1938

The play consists of three long spoken scenes, and, in addition, what I call the lyrical parts where we can have music, but very subdued, rather as it appears in the liturgy or in Erik Satie's *Socrate*. I should like to see inspiration rising from the murmur to the vowel, then the consonant, the word, the note, then finally to song and from thence descending again.

To Dullin he writes:

12 December 1938

Fix a day and a date for *Tobie*. I have a certain number of friends who would be interested in a reading. Don't forget that it brings in a great deal of music, mime and even cinema!

Present-day editions generally give the revised text, the "final version." The first version had the following general production note:

The idea behind the production is the constant use of slide and film projectors, which complete and throw into perspective the action carried on in the foreground by live characters. In the middle of the stage is a sort of raised tribune or platform reached by steps. A double chorus on each side of the stage comments on the action.

Some instructions about these projections were given with each scene. Finally one scene, which was kept in the final version, is entirely in dumb show.

ACT I
Scene VIII
THE ANGEL RAPHAEL
(Mime. Extremely slow)

1. The Angel comes down from heaven, his hands clasped above his head and his arms framing his face. Standing on the tips of his toes. Vertical.

2. With his arms bent in front of him, fingertips touching, he establishes the feeling of the horizontal.

3. With arms outstretched he gives an impression of instability, like a diver who has difficulty in keeping his balance in a denser environment.

4. With outstretched arms, a balancing movement is indicated. The fingertips quiver a little when the point of balance is reached (twice). The hands palms downward.

5. The left arm rises, the fingers taut, palm downward.
6. The right arm rises, the palm of the right hand upward.
7. The right hand comes to rest in the left hand. Balance as in 4, but palms upward.
8. Repeat 2.
9. Repeat 1.
10. Disappear.

In the 1942 edition, the first, this "prefatory note" appears, dated September 1938:

The stories, or parables, of the Old and New Testaments are not simply anecdotes to give the imagination a moment's entertainment. They have a character which I may call typical; I mean that they portray attitudes which are an essential and unchanging part of the human animal, that the events they show are perfect, and that they establish standards—themes of which everything which happens around us is only the development, partial illustration, or degeneration.

L'Histoire de Tobie et de Sara is an application of a sentence from the Gospel (Matt. 18:19–20): *If two of you shall agree on earth as touching any thing that they shall ask, it shall be done for them (fiet illis) of my Father which is in heaven. For where two or three are gathered together in my name, there am I in the midst of them.* Understand that this does not only mean a physical meeting. Christ speaks of a meeting in his name, of which he is the cause and the object, a common prayer, not only of the lips but of the heart, from people who are asking him for the same thing at the same time. These words remind us of those in Deuteronomy 13:15 quoted by St. Matthew and in the Second Epistle to the Corinthians: *in ore duorum vel trium testium stabit omne Verbum.* God wills that there should always be two witnesses, one on one side and one on the other, to establish the Word, which is the expression of a fact, and give it an objective value by means of a double testimony: this is what happened, this is the truth; we are two, each on his own side, to affirm and confirm it, and in our testimony we are one. We provide weight and counterweight, and the Word is there, standing firm in the middle. And what is true in the realm of fact has its counterpart in that of Charity. Every cry, every prayer, has an echo. When we speak directly to God, when we say yes one to the other, God lends an ear—if I dare say it—with both ears. *All the works of the Most High,* says Ecclesiasticus, *two and two, one against another.*

God ceaselessly commands us to pray, because he needs our prayers to take from him the weight of the mercy which guards the door of our heart until it opens, and of the milk he is ready to pour out for us. But the pleasure which prayer brings to God, and the intrinsic good of this personal act of love and trust do not react only on him who utters it. God never does good to one man alone. He never gives him anything which is not active and contagious. (That is what is meant by the word *fiet* which I have just emphasized, which reminds us of *fiat* in Genesis.) When we pray we give voice and expression to a wish or need which is not ours alone. We join someone else, known or unknown to us. We agree with him. We espouse his cause and reinforce it with ours. We give him practical help. Between us we set free the Spirit. We accomplish an act of brotherly and reciprocal charity which calls for and deserves a reward. For it is written (Matt. 25:40): *Inasmuch as ye have done it unto the least of these my brethren, ye have done it unto me.* God in his grace is pleased, then, to put on the garment of Justice, with the obligations it carries. We have come together before the Father in the name of Jesus to whom all things are possible. Jesus is the mediator through whom we have spoken together. He was there; he was that which spoke in all of us—the Son speaking to the Father through the Spirit. As he gives the answer, it is he who suggested the request and set flowing the current which carries our brother along with us.

Thus, at the same time, there is blind Tobit in Nineveh, persecuted by his wife and his household, and Sarah, daughter of Raguel at Rages, humiliated by her maidservant.

The interest of the Book of Tobit lies in the communion of these two souls in need, far apart and unknown to each other. This is the mainspring of the little "morality" which I wrote at the request of Mme. Ida Rubinstein, in which music, cinema, and mime come to the aid of the words. I know I shall be blamed for having taken certain liberties with the Biblical text, and for having laid such stress on the role of Sarah (representing for me the human soul) who is saved by Tobias, son of Tobit. I cut out Gabael, and made Raguel himself his relative's debtor, and trustee of the ten talents of silver. These represent the Scriptures, entrusted to the care of the Synagogue, which Tobias claimed on the authority of the "handwriting" which, St. Paul tells us, was nailed to the cross. Sarah does not follow her husband at a distance, but goes before him to the help of the blind man and his unhappy wife. The dramatist has his license as well as the painter.

It is also important to note that the story of Tobit is told in a large number of versions in various languages which show some remarkable differences. As Dom Calvet remarks in his Introduction: *But since in the different texts of the book we find speeches and descriptions of different lengths, we cannot be certain that the writers of the Holy Scriptures did not make various changes in terms and circumstances according to their own opinions and tastes, but without altering the basic story.*

10 September 1938

When the final text was published, Claudel added these few words, dated 7 April 1953.

This play was first conceived as a lyric drama in which music would have played an essential part. Reflection and experience have shown me that more room must be left for the dramatic element.

Theories Put Into Practice

During this period several of the early works were produced, some for the first time. Whenever Claudel was able to have a hand, he tried to make use of his recent discoveries.

L'Otage *at the Comédie-Française*

Claudel took very little part in rehearsals, but he intervened directly on one point, which he explained in *Excelsior* on 27 October 1934:

One of the unusual features of the production will be the spoken choruses in the first and third acts, for which I had the help of a great actress from Brussels, Mme. Renaud-Thevenet, who is particularly interested in this form of art, and has gathered around her a group of enthusiastic exponents. It was the Japanese theatre that gave me the idea. Between music and speech there is a whole domain, that of exclamation, which has hitherto not been used, and which offers the most interesting possibilities. Thanks to it I was able, in the first act of *L'Otage*, to give the impression of a stormy night much better than with mechanical means.

The Choephori *at Brussels*

On the subject of the "spoken choruses" of the *Choephori*, Claudel declared in an interview published in *Le Soir* on 21 March 1935:

This is really a new art we are discovering. Words are not strong enough to describe the passion with which Mme. Renaud is throwing herself into it, and I can't praise sufficiently the group of girls and boys among whom I have been working almost every day for several months. There are fifteen to twenty-five choral speakers, with four different types of voice, and they are giving the rhythm its rightful part. Rhythm, the succession of long and short vowels and the distribution of the stress accents are at least as important to poetry as the sense of the words. . . . That is what I tried to make clear in my translation of Aeschylus. I have attempted to adapt Greek meters to the French tongue. And Mme. Renaud's group has helped me more than I would have dared to hope.

We read in *La Nation belge* of 26 March 1935 yet another declaration:

In 1913 I made the acquaintance of Milhaud, and we understood each other at once. I perfected the *Choephori* during the hours of enforced leisure caused by the war. It was then that I discovered this progression from words to verse, from verse to chant, from chant to song, and from song to chorus. Later I put that into practice in *Christophe Colomb*. Cecilia de Vocht's admirable choir has already understood the importance of the chorus. The chorus is a living harp on which the actors play ceaselessly, making it a witness and an echo of the emotions they feel as the play progresses. Its conception rests upon a dialogue between witnesses.

L'Échange *at the Théâtre des Mathurins*

In this production Ludmilla Pitoëff played the part of Marthe. Ten years later, in 1947, when the play was revived, Claudel spoke of her thus:

Ludmilla Pitoëff never raises her voice very much, but no sooner has she begun to speak than her listener loses all desire to be anywhere but where he is. She reaches his very soul, and has discovered how to do it with the color and inflection of her voice. His ear still quivers with the echoes of a word just spoken, and he can only wait for the next with beating heart, watching for those lips to open again. But how she herself listens! how she sanctifies—if I may use the word—any words addressed to her! She impregnates them with such power of meaning and emotion, makes it so obvious that they are reaching their mark, simply by this deep attentiveness, this receptive silence. This is truth! Our eyes grow wet, and something awakens in our heart—something deep-seated, good, and genuine. "Poet, you explain nothing, but through you all things can be explained." I am fortunate beyond measure to have this lovely mouth explaining to me my own miserable weakness, with such sweet reason, and with that alternation of pitch that I know so well. And how beautiful the French language is on those faultless lips! There is such perfection in the way mind and voice combine to balance a sentence exactly, and in that infallible touch on a beautiful instrument that resounds so poignantly. There are no dreary alexandrines to force on us their irritating mathematical rhythm. There is only a soul, like a nightingale, inventing its rhythms as it sings. To us she is mother, lover, and finally Woman, strangely like the Wisdom of God!

And I have not even mentioned the slow perfection, the slow arrival at perfection, of attitudes and gestures, in consonance with the melody of her voice. Nor the measured movement like notes on a three-dimensional stave, aided by the authority of arm and hand. Nor those heartening gestures, born of true genius, which constitute almost an attack on those regions of our being in which our blind souls are guarding our most sacred treasures.

I knew Duse in her last years, and I do not think that in any of her public appearances she ever achieved anything comparable with that miracle of simplicity, sensitivity, and music which is our own Ludmilla Pitoeff.

Paris, 14 January 1947

L'Annonce faite à Marie

In 1938–1939, Copeau, and then Dullin, undertook to produce *L'Annonce faite à Marie* at the Comédie-Française. Both gave up the idea because of disagreements with Claudel. It is not very easy to deduce Claudel's tastes and demands at that particular moment from these refusals. It appears at least from the correspondence (*Cahier Claudel 6*) that he would not let Copeau use a symbolic set very like the Hellerau one, preferring a richer and more realistic décor. Dullin refused because Claudel had had a new choral score written for the play.

Copeau's notes tell us nothing about Claudel's intentions, but Jouvet kept the following notes taken during a conversation a little earlier.[11] This must have been in about 1930, when the Théâtre Pigalle had asked him to produce *L'Annonce faite à Marie:*

Act I:
  Set with a door
        a table
        a hearth, placed one above the other (the door being at the top, on the highest level)

Table: 16th century tomb
The father has certainly an enormous headdress
Costumes voluminous
Tomb at Philippi
Church of Brou
Act II:
The arrangement probably should not change, but we must give the impression of a garden, a sort of transparent stained-glass effect in pink and white (Sens Cathedral).
The whole background gray-white and pink.
Violaine in intense blue (alone).
With a wimple.
He cut holes in a sheet of paper and laid it on another sheet of paper and put it on the window where the light would shine through it to show me the translucent effect he wanted for the flowery garden (Japan). Filigree.
Act III:
The procession of the giants.
Abbey ruins.
Walls with openings.
He sees the figure of a saint covered with icicles.
Act IV:
Death scene arranged as in Act I.
Mara on guard alone.
The table waits like an empty altar.
Act V:*
The Cologne retable.
Primitive landscape.
Backcloth ultramarine. Sky red or green.
Below, the tomb.
When the cloth is spread or the shroud unfolded, the gesture is the same.
The Finale: white angels with velvet sleeves in green, blue, red, orange (see the angels of Melozzo da Forti).

* By this is probably meant the end of Act IV.

Theatre and Radio

On 30 September 1940, Claudel replied to an inquiry on literature organized by the *Figaro Littéraire*. One of the questions gave
him an opportunity to express his ideas on the theatre:

*In what order of importance do you place the different branches
of literature—novel, essay, criticism, poetry? Which do you think the
public should prefer?*

Your fifth question must be answered by everyone's personal tastes.
But when you listed the branches of literature you forgot two which,
though new, are already formidable rivals of both books and the
theatre. I mean radio and the cinema. It is no use hiding from ourselves
the fact that that is where the interests of the masses, and particularly
of young people, lie. It is a vivid, powerful, pressing, sweeping, tor-
rential reality, and they give it to you full in the face, at point-blank
range. You have no time to think, but no time to be bored either. In
comparison, the novel, with its endless leading up to the point, its constant appeal to the imagination, always begging our attention instead
of forcing itself on us, must seem so slow, diffuse, weak, and gloomy,
lost in a twilight distance! And how heavy and labored the theatre
appears, with its unsophisticated, unchanging set of which we tire in a
moment, its dialogue without thrills, its ceaseless tramping of feet, and
its faceless, unreal characters. The author has quite disappeared from
the screen, and what a relief!

But do not despair, unhappy scribbler! One new art has turned the
public's eye away from you, but another is at your side ready to lend an
ear. All that white paper with your very soul lying on it in black lines
and dots was in fact a gag. Now it is gone, and instead an immense

audience is handed over to you. You can reach them directly: they will be affected by the very tone of your voice; the outpourings of your mind are free to flow into other minds without any barrier between. Language returns to the place from which it was ousted by literature. It flies on wings to our understanding—and what more appropriate vehicle for thought than the waves of the ether! Some poor hacks have gone on for so long with impunity that they have become as deaf as posts. But the gibberish of, say, Sainte-Beuve (who has only too many imitators today) would paralyze the microphone before it ever had the chance to assail the listeners' ears. The poet, orator, interpreter, commentator, or agitator is no longer alone. He is two people, not one, and he has a world at his disposal and the whole planet to echo his words. He can fling his message to the farthest horizon, and is that not better than filling gloomy pages to be entombed within the covers of a book?

Do not misunderstand me. I still believe in the force of the written word, and I know there is magic in the dark liquid that flows from a fountain pen. The gods, as our ancestors said, or, quite simply, men, events, nature, the past, the present, the future, all need an interpreter, well prepared, patient, and careful, to grasp their *meaning* and hold it safe. And if we love an author, we do not want merely to indulge in him for a few minutes; we want to possess him. We want to adopt and adapt him, and to do this in all the various facets of our temperament, judgment, and personality, we need time. We like to have him as a permanent guest on our library shelves. But there is no reason why the spoken word should not be his herald.

And since I have just mentioned the theatre, and shall return to it later, the resources of radio drama are immense. It is a concert of souls, a clash of wills, presented to us in the absolute, free from the clumsiness of bodily movements. Who knows? This, rather than the mummified exhibitions we are used to, may be our classical theatre in its perfect form, the only form in which it is capable of surviving. And what a feeling of security, when we can stretch out a finger and stop the interminable discourses of Berenice and Antiochus!

However, I am not condemning the stage any more than books. There is always the hope that one day it may be revolutionized once more by some man of genius. What should we do without the actor or actress, there before our eyes, alive and passionately involved in his part, no reflection but an independent source of ideas and emotions? And how can we give him back his indispensability in this world that science has let loose upon us, insubstantial, glamorous, and on its own somewhat disappointing? Wagner sought in vain for a perfect agreement between words and music; a similar harmony between drama and the commentary which cinema and radio can provide for it is the ideal toward which we are vaguely groping—and what problems this is going to pose for the art of the future! Not to speak of French verse-speaking which we shall have to study on a truer basis once those appalling alexandrines no longer sound false notes in our ears. Nor the vast and almost unexplored domain of gesture, attitude, and choral speaking.

Public money would be far better spent on encouraging the seekers and pioneers of new art rather than on perpetuating those graveyards, the subsidized theatres. When you look back, as you can at my age, at the history of the arts over the last fifty years, you realize that the role of these sinister establishments has been no more than that of a refrigerator. Everything of any real interest that has happened in the theatre has been done by private enterprise, often in pathetically poor conditions. I am thinking of the Russian and Swedish ballets, the Vieux-Colombier, and such heroes as Lugné-Poe and our beloved Pitoeff. *Cyrano de Bergerac* was produced at Porte-Saint-Martin and *L'Aiglon* at the Théâtre Sarah-Bernhardt. During this time, the Théâtre-Français was reviving *Britannicus*, putting on *Le Marquis de Priola*, and offering us, for our amusement, the antics of M. de Pourceaugnac.

We are lucky at the moment in having an artist of genius from whom we can expect great things. I mean Jean-Louis Barrault. I went several times to see the two plays he created last year at the Atelier—*Hamlet* and *La Faim*. It was really remarkable. But alas! I have just read that he has been engaged for the Théâtre-Français and given a small part in *Le Misanthrope*. Ye Gods—*Le Misanthrope!* Let us hope that he escapes out of that straitjacket in time!

Brangues, 30 September 1940

Part III

The Plays Produced

Le Soulier de satin

Claudel discovered Jean-Louis Barrault in 1939, and immediately wanted him to direct and star in one of his plays:

25 April 1939

You are an amazing actor, and I have been looking for you all my life! You realize that an actor should play not only with his eyes and tongue, but with his whole body, using all the infinite potentialities for self-expression which the human body possesses.

This collaboration did not take place until 1943. Claudel was then living at Brangues, but he had long conversations with his producer on several occasions. We can look for information in at least a few letters and other writings:[1]

29 April 1943

My dear B.,

I would like you to send me the sketches for the women's costumes. I found some quite suitable costumes in *Larousse du XXᵉ siècle*. See for example, under *Florinetta*.

Also the plate *"Costumes."* A Mary Stuart type headdress for Doña Honoria?

For the Neapolitan sergeant see *Règne d'Henri III*. The little cape is very amusing.

For the women (Doña Sept-Épées?) the little cap with a feather at the side is rather sweet.

Best wishes,

P. Claudel.

8 June 1943

My dear B.,

Your letter has prepared me for disillusionment when I next get to Paris, but I know the theatrical world well enough to realize that most of the useful work is generally done at the last minute. You are the one who counts. I am so sorry I didn't manage to see you. I wanted to talk to you about this question of the Moon and the Double Shadow. For the Moon, C's idea is impossible—she looks like a carnival queen. I have a good though difficult plan, but I should have to show you my sketches. I'm thinking hard about the Double Shadow. Human figures would be too lumpish and solid. Only the cinema can give me the poetic quality I want. I imagine the bodies as sketchy as possible, but the hands and arms very precise and detailed.

One arm and hand—the man's—rising slowly throughout the whole scene, and another hand—the woman's—coming down on to it, covering it, closely intertwining with it. Then the man's hand is slowly disengaged and moves downward, following the outline of the woman's body, while her arm is extended, waving gently like a palm frond in the light, and her head droops heavily, like a fruit, on the other side. . . . For the feeling of the thing, I would like you to look at a magnificent marble group by my sister Camille which is at Mme. Berthelot's (13 boulevard des Invalides). She will be pleased to show it to you.

Brangues, 9 October 1943

Dear Rodrigo,

I have just finished reading the proofs of *Le Soulier de satin* (Comédie-Française edition) and I found your stage directions very amusing. But now there are quite a lot of alterations to make; I suppose you have already started work on them? It would be a good thing if the book could come out as soon as possible as the old edition is now unobtainable. I see no need to add Honegger's music, which would only make the book too big and too expensive. I'm very sorry to leave out the brambles, the court scene behind the transparent curtain on the Fourth Day (the Death's head) and most, most, most of all the *Double Shadow*. It is absolutely necessary to see these lovers united in a common shadow or image before seeing them separated in the Moon scene. Don't worry about V's opinion—we have already seen that his taste is not perfect. It is annoying to have failed to carry out our ideas, and this is the only time it has happened! I think that the Shadow on a screen is the best thing on the whole, but we ought to make use of the cinema. I did not insist because I didn't like the way it was done. The right note is not violence but a *poignant sweetness* which should be heartrending (and we should actually see the Shadow torn apart before our eyes). And the effect of two spoken voices together is confused and *ugly*. We need singing, but as near as possible to speech, with very slight inflections and cadences. Discuss the problem with our friend H. It's difficult, but it will be interesting to look for a solution. This thorny problem of marrying music and speech is still with us, but *Le Soulier* has taken us a step further, and no mistake. . . .

A little later Claudel came back to the problem with his usual stubbornness.

29 February 1944

It's settled then—I'll keep my promise and I shall be there for the fiftieth performance with all my valiant cast. . . . I'm still eaten up with regret over the *Double Shadow*. The more I think of it, the more I see that we needed that scene. It is annoying for both of us to have been beaten by material considerations. Could we really not look at the matter again? If we could do it, it would add to the interest of subsequent performances. . . .

PROBLEMS OF DICTION

Brangues, 22 June 1944

Dear Barrault,

Since you are interested—and rightly so—in questions of diction, I am sending you an extract from a preface by Bergson to a collection of speeches made in America by the orator Viviani:[2]

"By what magic did M. Viviani captivate and carry away his listeners, many of whom did not know French? It happened every time, always going through the same phases. From the very first words, the audience leaned almost physically toward him, letting itself go with the music of his speech. As the orator became more animated and *his gestures showed his thought and emotion more forcibly* (the underlining is mine) the audience was drawn into this movement, took over the rhythm of his emotion, fell into step with his thought, and understood the gist of the phrase even when they did not understand the words. But soon the words began to have meaning, because terms common to both languages, or proper names with a ring of glory, shone out now and then, shedding their glow over everything between, like the lights outlining some monuments on festival days, when a few lamps here and there, with the help of the wind, suddenly illuminate the whole. This, I think, was the explanation of the magic by which M. Viviani's thought was directly communicated, without an intermediary, to the minds of others."

Another passage is more valuable because it gives a minutely detailed commentary on a few sentences in *Le Soulier de satin*:[3]

I am sure the actors have perfected their diction. Nevertheless, I have some remarks to make to X and Y who still tend to bellow from time to time.

X

Flamboya͞nte dans le so͞uffle du Saint-Espirit.
No, no, no!
Straight off, without hesitation, and accentuated by the arms held vertically (together, not outspread) in a single column ascending like a rocket, with the fingers pointed.
F̲lamboyante dans le sou̲ffle du Saint-Espirit. The whole impetus given by the initial F̲l further accentuated by the second, the body participating, from the loins and the calves.
Une etoi̲lle
F̲f lamboyante
In sou̲ffle, on the other hand, it is the *l* which gives the force (odd!)
The *r* of Esprit is important.
Bear this in mind.

The same

Au revoir, soeur chérie, dans la lumi͞ère éterne͞lle.
Very bad fault (these two sounds have nothing like the same value!)
Au revoi̲r, soeu̲r c̲h̲érie.
Four *r*'s, but the fourth must for the sake of expression take second place to the tender, caressing c̲h̲.
Dans la l̲lumi̲ère é te̲r'nelle.
The impetus and enthusiasm are furnished by the initial *l. ère* is important but owes its force to the *r* repeated in éte̲r-nelle.

Half-sigh after *mière* and *éter*.

On *ter*, slight drawing out, and slight sharpening of the voice, fading on *nelle*.

The melody is very delicate, resting on a vowel as colorless as *e*. The two open *e*'s in *ère* and *ter* are not exactly the same.

It is a curious fact that it is the consonant which gives the timbre of the vowel!

But X must not worry about these subtleties. The important thing is the impetus on the *l* of lumière.

Now for Y

I can't go into details because the music rather got in the way, but I am sure that it is wrong to say with a succession of equal stresses (Mounet-Sully style):

. . . vers <u>moi</u> le grand Ap<u>ô</u>tre du Firm<u>ame</u>nt qui ex<u>iste</u> dans cet <u>éta</u>t de transp<u>or</u>t.

What is the central idea, emphasized by the speaker's gigantic stature?

<u>Mm</u>oi <u>le</u> <u>grand</u> Ap<u>ô</u>tre <u>du</u> <u>F</u>irmament.

That's the strong point. The F is a powerful message to base. Firmament: brilliantly, indestructibly secure, affirmed by the F, and confirmed by the two equal syllables: Manman. It has thus a great deal of authority.

<u>Qui existe dans cet état de transport</u>

is very mysterious despite the flash of light [*or*] on the final syllable. What does it mean?

It is the same idea as that expressed by the Jesuit Father:

Ce qu'il essayera misérablement de dire sur la terre, je suis là pour le traduire dans le ciel.

St. James is a sort of supernatural device for transporting things from one world to the other, from earth to heaven, from fact to meaning. (That is his reason for existing.)

That is why we have the four *t*'s (5 with the *d*, not 6!) qui ex<u>iste</u> <u>d</u>ans ce<u>t</u> <u>éta</u>t <u>d</u>e <u>t</u>ransp<u>or</u>t.

So you must say, lowering your voice after firmam., and articulating by syllables:

Qui exi<u>ste</u> <u>d</u>ans ce<u>t</u> <u>éta</u>t <u>d</u>e <u>t</u>rans p<u>ó</u>rt!

The final *or* thus flashes out to make a magnificent ending, like a star!

As a general rule, every actor at the Th.-Fr. must ask himself, "What would Mounet-Sully have done in my place?" (He had a magnificent temperament, nevertheless!)

And don't do it!

On the First Performance of the Soulier de satin at the Théâtre-Français

Stunned and moved beyond words, I have just left the first rehearsal of the Soulier de satin that I have been able to attend. I feel like one of those Renaissance monks thrust back by an order from the Pope into the tumult of the outside world. I have been abruptly torn away from my long solitude in the valley of the Rhône, thrust into the depths of that secluded and secret cavern they call a theatre, and allowed to see something that existed for so long only in my imagination, blown up to life-size, speaking and moving. It has not yet come completely to life. It stammers, takes its first tottering steps; hands grope for each other, lands and palaces fall from heaven, the right side finds itself at the beginning of what belongs to the left side. An industrious multitude swarms like an anthill in the half-darkness pierced by the beam of a spotlight. A multitude set in motion by the bold resolution of the general director, M. Jean-Louis Vaudoyer, and given life and impetus, from the humblest stagehand to the characters on the stage whose task it is to bring the action to its close, by the mind of the producer, Jean-Louis Barrault, to whom I have entrusted my work, knowing that his artistic convictions are identical with mine.

In a few days the public will share my experience. It will not see a finished product, a text recited turn by turn. Materially and spiritually, the work will be born and grow before its eyes.

In the meantime, I am the only guest here in the depths, and the task of contemplation is mine. I am, so to speak, installed in the future, waiting for the scenes which follow one another to the end to appear behind me. Here the action cannot take advantage of a site prepared for something else. From top to bottom, from left to right, the various elements join together to suck into themselves like a whirlpool both actors and play. But, as we all confusedly feel, is that not how things happen in real life? Are we not all waiting for the pitiless summons of the stage manager, commanding our entrances and exits in this play going on around us? The moment has come!

For we are not meant to carve out our destiny alone. We are allotted our place in an undertaking. We are needed to give a sort of interpretation or intelligible account of a situation. We have been entrusted with the performance, together with partners who reveal themselves to us one after the other, of a kind of huge parable in which the most secret and sensitive fibers of our being are involved for the greater glory of God. But *The worst may never happen.*

The play is only the means by which the event, the moment of change, the essential and central conflict on which all human life is based, is isolated, outlined, completed, illustrated, and given its place in the domain of both the general and the particular. It takes a certain potential for contradiction among the forces present, and transforms it into action in order to reach a conclusion.

What are these forces in *Le Soulier de satin?*

They are the most primitive ones between which the human heart has ever been torn. On the one hand, the passionate longing for individual happiness in which the most austere of philosophies recognizes not only the mainspring but the legitimate aspiration of all our energies, conscious or unconscious; and on the other hand, the external necessity to which this desire has to adapt itself. When these two forces, both— and I say it without hesitation—sacred, come into conflict, there is a problem to solve, and a solution to find; there is drama. If there is no conflict, there is nothing to settle.

This is the meaning of the reply I once gave to M. André Gide's famous quip: *Good literature was never made with good sentiments.* Not with good sentiments alone, perhaps (but what does that mean anyway?) but still less with bad ones. There is nothing less dramatic, duller, and less interesting than the instinct that takes the quickest route to its own satisfaction. If this deep-seated longing for good which is within us—and can be called animal just as well as moral—is deprived of the firm shape which opposition imparts to it, we are left with a vague insipid mass floating in a vacuum, or the bitter repression of the spectator's conscience, which is nothing without protest. Without good, and without the desire for good, there can be no evil. Without good sentiments, there can be no bad ones. And without struggle, there can be no progress.[4]

Le Soulier de satin *and the Public*
Written by Paul Claudel after the fiftieth performance
of the play (Brangues, Maundy Thursday 1944)

I have just attended the fiftieth performance of *Le Soulier de satin*, and it gave me a better opportunity than the earlier performance to observe the reactions of the audience which, for four months, has never failed to fill to the brim the great bowl of our national theatre in order to see the play. Someone somewhere has spoken of the power of aspiration of characters and events wielded by the set which we see coming down from the flies and opening out from both the left and right sides at the same time, put together and taking shape before the eyes of the audience. But I think the play itself wields this same power of attraction over this mass of people, both men and women, who have flocked here from every corner of France and every rank of society. It is like a sort of vacuum working. All these various beings have given up their own preoccupations and personalities. For their own words they have substituted those of the poet. All are silent and attentive, in a strange state of collective sensitivity and magnetic communication.

If I try to analyze the reason for this fascination which makes a crowd of people, generally considered as frivolous, follow a play of which the first part alone lasts two and a half hours on end, without tiring or letting their attention wander, and even with a feeling of regret when it is over, I think first of the variety of types of scene, few of which last longer than about ten minutes. There is no time to be bored. Something new and unexpected is always happening.

Then—and it was a doctor who made this ingenious suggestion—people know the play will be long, and prepare for it psychologically, as they would for a long journey. Too short a play would not give the enchantment time to work. Our resistance is not overcome. We are only half there, and we have left someone outside who calls impatiently to us the whole time.

And then, the poet has the reputation of being a difficult author. There is a triple advantage to be gained from that. First, the spectator has made an honest attempt to get into a receptive frame of mind. He is ready. He has brought all his intelligence and goodwill to bear. In the second place, he is agreeably surprised to find that it is all happening quite painlessly, and not only is he not suffering, not only is he interested; he is enjoying himself. And in the third place, he is pleased both with himself and with the author who has given him a good opinion of his own tastes and intelligence and the opportunity to justify them. We ask a great deal of the public, so why should we doubt that it is ready to give it? It can see that the poet for his part has not spared himself and has done all he could.

Are these reasons enough to explain everything? Is it simply a professional matter—the skill of the dramatist, the producer, the scenic designer, the composer, and those incomparably talented actors? Is it simply the satisfaction of a superficial curiosity? Or is it perhaps that there on the stage, where the parable is unfolding in all its solemnity, a subject is being debated which reaches down to the deepest, most sacred recesses of our humanity, and speaks to the soul, to that child of God that every man must always be, whether he will or no? It speaks perhaps to that part deep within us which knows our right to love, to transcendent happiness, and to something outside ourselves, the lack of which is our deepest misfortune, and for which we long forever in despair and bitter nostalgia.

And here we realize to the full the idea of *aspiration*, of the whirlpool *sucking* everything into itself, which I suggested in the first lines of this essay. What dramatic poet has never been driven to envy and even despair by the name of Shakespeare? It is true that in France we have Racine, who, on another plane—his own—can almost counterbalance the giant from across the Channel. From the point of view of the composition, of the intrinsic relationship of the components, the logical analysis of the passions involved and the perfection of their expression, the Globe Theatre has never done anything comparable with *Britannicus*, *Phèdre*, and *Athalie*. Shakespeare never drew female characters with the delicacy, wit, dignity and inward intensity of Phèdre, Agrippine, Andromaque, Roxane, and Iphigénie. What the French dramatist lacks in verbal imagination he makes up for by the polished beauty of his language and by that undying quality which the Greeks call *to prepon*. And yet we cannot deny that the Englishman's empire extends its frontiers much farther than the artificially enclosed arena of the pupil of Port-Royal. Faced with that feeling for nature, that vitality in every character down to the most unimportant, that overflowing gaiety, those constant surprises that genius has in store for us, that inexhaustible freedom which brings together the various parts of the action, not like spokes from a circumference but like rivers drawn by a common center of gravity—faced with all this, who would not share the enthusiasm of Berlioz?

And yet . . . And yet a Christian, a Catholic, I mean a complete man, cannot feel satisfied even with the work of Shakespeare. The old Greek theatre, that of Aeschylus, Sophocles, and even Euripides—I say nothing of its incomparably superior style—had a higher ideal. Shakespeare's world lacks . . . what? The most important part, heaven, the third dimension, the Vertical. We are entertained, interested, filled with enthusiasm, but we are never gripped, seized by the throat, faced by a pitiless Sphinx to whom we must reply, as we are, for example, by

Antigone, or Cassandra, or Alcestis. On the plane of fact, bounded by the horizon, it is impossible to imagine anything richer, more intelligent, more diverting, more dramatic, more illuminating, more suggestive. But afterward, all these people go about their business and are still subject to the laws of gravity. They are never called upon to transcend themselves. What have I to do with them? And sometimes we are ashamed to feel Hamlet's words breathed softly from our own lips: "Man delights not me! no, nor woman neither."

And here the advantage is with an old dramatist whom some people have long been foolish enough to compare with great Racine, and even to prefer him. I mean Corneille. Certainly no words are harsh enough to describe this hard-faced old fossil who, in his laboriously versified dramatic "cases," thought he could make up by a lawyer's cleverness and fluency what he lacked in poetic genius. When we see a man like Péguy growing excited over a play like *Polyeucte*, which he considers a masterpiece of Christian tragedy, we are amazed. If there ever was a complete and utter pagan, imbued to the very marrow with the kind of politics we now call realistic, with pride and a false semblance of honor as his only morals, foreign to any ideas of charity or humility, in whom the university pedant, puffed up with the wind of Graeco-Latin sophistry, was superimposed on the most overstuffed of provincial bourgeois, it was this Peter, brother of Thomas. But let us do justice to this repellent figure. He was the only one to reintroduce to the theatre the grandiose idea of sacrifice, with its ritual and religious associations, the only one to consider dramatic action as bringing out in man not only what is most characteristic and most picturesque in him, but also what is most noble and most representative. A pure breath, that of heroism in default of sanctity, blows from time to time over these stridently screeching characters—an appeal to the soul. What a pity they never lose their passion for attitudinizing, and that this pupil of the Jesuits never knew any other morals but those of the old dotard of Chaeronea.[5]

And then, since you have asked me to, why should I not be imprudent enough to talk about myself, and say quite boldly that this idea of sacrifice, of refusing immediate benefits for eternal ones, is the life-force of all the plays of P. C., who, ladies and gentlemen, will soon have the right to sign P. P. C.?[6] And this P. C. has never considered dramatic action, Spanish or otherwise, as anything but a complex device to bring out the most essential in a character—the image of God or of the adversary of God. Each character answers his personal call, and answers it with a name—his own. *Adsum!* Sacrifice creates a sort of vacuum, and lays us open by an act of will to the purest elements of our liberty. It calls into being that which is divine to us. We abdicate voluntarily and give place to an action arising from the Grace of God; we join forces with the Almighty to our immense advantage. Rodgrigo and Prouhèze part, but Rodgrigo creates a world, and Prouhèze saves another—the world which is enclosed in a man's soul.

THE PART PLAYED BY THE SET

These performances of *Le Soulier de satin* appear to have led Claudel to discover a new aspect of the theatre—the décor. Up to this point, he had considered it rather as a painter than as a dramatist. He wrote to Lucien Coutaud, who designed the sets for *Le Soulier*, a few days after the performance:

I have particularly high praise for the sets because I feel they too are conceived as a dramatic rather than a pictorial element. I expect you have read my very important article in *Comoedia*, and realized my interest in the dynamic role played for the first time by the décor in *Le Soulier*, and how it served as center of attraction for all the other elements. The audience sees the action beforehand in its lines and planes, its architecture and its colors, as the plan of a church depends on the services to be held in it. The set depends on the actions about to be carried out in it, and to which it offers its possibilities. Thank you for having understood that. . . .

The article in *Comoedia* is the first of the two preceding ones. Claudel never forgot this lesson. He applied it, as we shall see later, to *L'Annonce faite à Marie*, to all the second versions (cf. Introduction) written in the next few years, and to the production of *Partage de midi*. He remembered it on the occasions when he undertook dramatic criticism. For instance, he wrote about *King Lear*:[7]

The sets are the kind to which it is impossible to make any objection, except that they would do just as well for any other play. Sets do not play a purely occasional part. *They don't simply happen.*[8] The action should appear to create them, and they in their turn are there to give it coherence and support. In *King Lear*, the palaces of the two daughters, at whose doors the unhappy father knocks, to be rejected by each in turn, should have been placed symmetrically. We could have seen him, miserably trudging between the two. Similarly, in the mad scenes there should have been a touch of madness in the décor. Could we not have had some sinister ruin such as Victor Hugo might have imagined?

Christophe Colomb

The Man Who United the Earth, Christopher Columbus[9]

I. The crews are recruited

1. The scene begins with the recruitment of crews for the expedition. The police search prisons (the man condemned to death), inns, houses of ill repute, etc. A woman informs on her husband and the husband on his wife's lover. All are carried away. The recruits are gathered together in a public square. Their trouser buttons have been cut off so that they cannot run away. Off they go! The drum rolls, the trumpet sounds, the flag is unfurled! The bells are heard dimly in the distance! At the head of the column the Leader, somewhat tattered, rides a very skinny horse.

The Embarkation

2. The port. The three caravels. Boats loaded with civil, military, and religious officials, provisions, etc. The boats with the recruits can be seen. Exchange of gibes. Officials climb on board up the ladder.

Waiting for Christopher Columbus

3. The deck of the *Santa Maria* with all the visitors waiting impatiently. Where is Christopher Columbus? He is late!

He appears!
(I should prefer 16th century costumes)

4. He is alone in a little boat, extremely tall and thin, austere-looking. With him, the fat jovial cook. Rather the idea of Don Quixote and Sancho Panza. Kitchen equipment, provisions, watermelons, flasks of wine, etc. The cannon thunders. Christopher Columbus, whose back was turned at first, is now facing the public. He makes a wide slow gesture of salute with his hat.

II. *Interlude*

1. Tumult. Enter Producer No. 2, the staff trying in vain to hold him back; people and equipment are pushed around. The organizer, through carelessness or indifference, has commissioned two rival producers. Producer No. 1 is stupefied. No. 2 has a rag which he dips into the sea on the screen. He wrings it out and tries to wipe out with it the picture of Christopher Columbus, with only partial success because it always reappears.

Christopher in the Azores. The old sailor

2. PRODUCER NO. 1: Give me your rag, and we'll see if I have better luck! He succeeds in wiping out the picture.
The screen is blank, and all at once music comes out of it!
PRODUCER NO. 2, *sneering:* Music! But it isn't even music . . .
    (Musical interlude)
PRODUCER NO. 1: Watch! Music and vacancy are giving birth to something.
    Gradually, the picture of a wreck takes shape on the screen (bowsprit, figurehead, etc.). An old sailor is clinging to it, nearly dead. Christopher Columbus questions him.
    (Chorus)
There is land to the West! There is land to the West!

Why the mule?

3. The director loses his patience and yells an order to the cameraman. The scene is cut.
It's my turn!
    Rumbling of machinery, flashes, and then suddenly there appears on the screen. . . .
    A MULE! Christopher Columbus' mule.

PRODUCER NO. 1, *convulsed with laughter:* A mule—isn't it a scream? What's a mule doing here?
PRODUCER NO. 2: So what? We've got a bit muddled, that's all. Anyway that mule's more important than you think. You'll see!

But we must start at the beginning. What you're going to see is the Creation.

A whistle is blown.

The screen is blank.

The Creation

(Music)
4. Two gigantic hands appear on the screen. They dip into a bucket containing a luminous material which they knead into a ball. Above them there appears in a frame a kind of list (lines in Hebrew characters). These are the specifications for the creation of the world. Articles 1, 2, 3, 4, etc. A forefinger is seen moving from one to the other. Then the hands reappear. The ball flies from one to the other. Suddenly it remains motionless, suspended. Then slowly it begins to turn by itself. Seas and continents take shape on its surface, becoming more detailed at each revolution. Finally, the American continent appears. The ball stops turning, and above it, in the frame, appear the two fateful letters:

O. K.

III. *St. James*

1. Christopher Columbus has left for his great adventure. But he needs prayers to breathe on him and waft him in the right direction across the measureless abyss. Which characters in our film are going to provide these prayers? Each of the producers has his own ideas on this subject. But they agree on one point. They both want St. James the Apostle, the patron saint of Spain, St. James the pilgrim who must also be the patron saint of this adventure, Columbus' guide across the boundless distance, St. James who for centuries had drawn all Christendom toward his shrine. [Here, perhaps, we could see a street in Paris, the Rue Saint-Jacques with pilgrims, men and women, wearing wide-brimmed hats with cockleshells, carrying staves, and walking (animals, baggage, sick people).]

Now we see St. James' shrine, an altar with a colossal statue in baroque style (never mind about the anachronism) turned toward the setting sun. Christopher Columbus is praying there before leaving, and we see his three caravels, reduced in size, at his feet.

Those who pray for Christopher Columbus

2. Each of the producers leads on by the hand the suppliant he has chosen.

Producer No. 1 brings on Queen Isabella, gorgeously dressed, and settles her on a prie-Dieu in front of the altar.

(He arranges her train, and since he is pleased with his idea, he stands triumphantly beside her. He takes a pinch of snuff. Then, on second thought, he too kneels. He puts his handkerchief on the ground to kneel on.)

Spain has just won back all her former territory. Europe has been freed from the Moslem yoke. Now the conquerors' ambition extends beyond the limits of the old horizons. St. James, faithful pilgrim, follower of the setting Sun who goes before to trace your path, guide our champion to the longed-for shores! The earth must be reunited with itself, and the conquest of the *ring* accomplished. The whole earth under God's sun must at last deserve the name of *catholic* (universal).

Those who pray for Christopher Columbus

3. But Producer No. 2 brings other suppliants to St. James. They are Christopher Columbus' creditors, who have paid for the expedition and are in great need of their money. They come in picturesque array, with lighted candles in their hands. (One of the candles goes out. The Producer relights it with a taper. One of the children is not paying attention. The Producer looks at him reproachfully and shows him how to pray, putting on a sanctimonious air and folding his hands.)

The creditors. They kneel behind Isabella and howl in pitiful voices: (Suitable music)

Grand saint Jacques, con-dui-sez Christophe Colomb!

Grand saint Jacques, ramenez-nous Christophe Colomb qui là-bas est parti a la recherche de notre argent.[10]

One of the creditors stands up and shows his empty pockets.

St. James towing the fleet

4. Here the whole building and the statue itself split into two. The two

halves open like doors, showing, as far as the eye can see, the Ocean lit by the full moon.

St. James steps forward, like a Colossus. The sea comes up to his loins, and he has the Pillars of Hercules on his shoulder. He is pulling Christopher Columbus' three caravels by a thread. In the sky are the three stars in a diagonal line called *Orion's Belt* and also *St. James's Staff*.

The mutiny

5. The sky becomes overcast. Thunder rumbles. The expedition has reached the part of the Atlantic near the Equator, called the Pitch Pot. The sailors, terrified by the persistent wind that drives them westward, have mutinied and are trying to force their admiral to return.

For the words of the play, see the book.

This is my idea:

I want the same effect as with a storm beginning. A sudden flash of lightning showing everything with dazzling clarity for a second, then complete and utter darkness.

The dialogue between Columbus and the mutinous sailors will be heard in the darkness. Then the scene will appear in a flash of lightning, and the boat will plunge into darkness again, with the dialogue still continuing.

Various scenes of the mutiny. Sailors crowded on the yards and ladders, some with guns, some negroes. The cook making encouraging grimaces out of his porthole.—Christopher Columbus seen for a second, immensely tall and white—On another boat, the rival only waiting for a sign to take over the command, etc.

Perhaps at one point the colossal form of St. James outlined in black?

Land!

6. See the book.

Daybreak. Birds fly into the rigging. The outline of land appears. The chaplain comes on, and is quickly given his vestments and the book. A candle is lit. *Te Deum!* Everyone kneels. But the cook is not happy. Christopher Columbus draws a sword above the priest.

The land is coming very near, and we can see nothing else. It has taken on the shape of a woman lying with her breasts pointing upward, a horn of plenty in her arms (see Jean Charlot's drawing).

Christopher Columbus appears in black, very small, in one of the woman's hands, kneeling, holding the Banner of Christ.

(Two possible pictures. We can see that enormous hand in which he is kneeling.)

The cook

7. The cook in the prow of the ship, alone, looking out, with obvious displeasure, a hand shading his eyes. He is carrying a saucepan.

We can hear *vaguely the muffled echoes of the* Te Deum.

IV. Controversy

1. Christopher Columbus' discovery has sent a wave of emotion throughout the world, especially the academic world. We see a huge hall with a lecturer's desk at one end, and behind it a large map of the world as it was known at that time. All sorts of strange instruments: telescopes, astrolabes, globes, armillary spheres, desks, huge books, documents with seals, etc.

Learned men are quarreling, seizing each other by the beard or the nose, yelling Greek words and proper names: Ptolemée! Anaxagore! A-na-ximandre! One signals to another in the distance to come to his help.

(In close-up, a large nose with spectacles on it, grasped by a thumb and forefinger which are pulling it.)

In the middle of all this, a young boy sitting on a table swinging his legs and calmly munching an apple.

The three wise men

2. At the Spanish court. See the book. The Three Wise Men are discussing with the King (very Greek) what is to be done with Christopher Columbus who is becoming an embarrassment. This scene must be entirely musical, with the effect of a grotesque ballet.

The conspiracy

3. At Hispaniola, darkness lit by one lamp. The conspirators have just received orders to seize Christopher Columbus and bring him back to

Spain in chains. Glasses and bottles. The cook is listening. A bat flies in above them and puts out the lamp.

The arrest

4. We see the officer giving Christopher Columbus notice of his arrest. The soldiers lay hands on him. But no one will put on the chains. The cook undertakes this. On hands and feet. Embarkation. Perhaps a Caribbean woman with a child in her arms weeps and clings to him.

The gods churn up the sea

5. On one side we see the gods of Africa and on the other the gods of America, perched on each other's shoulders, signaling to each other. They had let Christopher Columbus pass the first time because St. James was too strong for them. But this time they determined not to let him return. The tug of war begins.

Heave-oh! Heave-oh!

The storm begins. Thunderclaps.

The gods who are churning up the sea suddenly appear in a lightning flash, streaming with water.

The storm

6. a) Christopher Columbus is seen chained to the foot of the main-mast, in the light of a lantern which dances as the ship rolls. The captain and the officers take him on deck.

b) In a flash of lightning we see the tug-of-war line between the two teams of demons.

The prow of the caravel appears, and on it Christopher Columbus, gigantic, still with the cook beside him.

c) He raises his manacled hands and cries out:

There was a man called Christopher Columbus!

The line breaks in a crash of thunder.

The teams of demons on both sides fall over backward. Calm returns little by little.

The moon shines, and loud mutterings are heard: *There was a man called Christopher Columbus! There was a man called Christopher Columbus!*

V. *Christopher Columbus mocked*

1. Christopher Columbus has returned to Spain. He tries to get back into the King's favor, but is not received. He has to pay someone to introduce him.

Ballet, a quadrille in which the ladies are Pride, Stupidity, Ignorance and Greed. (No need for symbolic costumes.) Among the male dancers is a dwarf (the Marquis of Villaloba). At each pause in the dance, the Introducer presents Christopher Columbus to one of the ladies, who pretends to welcome him, then turns her back, sneering.

Christopher Columbus at the inn at Valladolid with his mule

2. Christopher Columbus is ill at the inn. He has nothing left. He looks in his chest and finds only chains. He hangs them on the wall.

The innkeeper demands his money. Christopher Columbus shows him his chains.

But he has one thing left after all—his old Mule. She puts her nose round the door to see if she can come in. Christopher Columbus takes his hat off to her and begs her to be seated.

Conversation with the Mule. Christopher Columbus tells her his troubles. The Mule listens graciously. Christopher Columbus asks her advice; he puts on his spectacles and reads papers to her. The Mule says yes and no, lowers first one ear, then the other, tries to scratch herself with her hind hoof.

The innkeeper returns with the police to demand his money. They try to lay hands on Christopher Columbus. But the Mule chases them away.

The end is near

3. Queen Isabella is dead. Her soul has taken the shape of a tiny girl (like a Velasquez Infanta). All her court, too, have become like children. The whole scene is white and silver, pointed here and there by pink and green. Music like tinkling glass.

Sultan Miramolin (also a child) brings her the keys of Granada (representing Paradise).

And Christopher Columbus? What has happened to Christopher Columbus?

(Flashback to the inn at Valladolid and the scene with the Mule.)
Poor Christopher Columbus!
He has suffered enough! O God, deliver Christopher Columbus!

O God, deliver Christopher Columbus!

4. The sky above the sea at sunset. The characters of the last scene are silhouetted, very small, against a background consisting of a narrow black band lit by the red flames of the candles they are holding in their hands.
Night falls. The stars appear. They are all the souls in this world to be, the world Christopher Columbus has discovered.
They pray for Christopher Columbus.

The bound hands

5. But God's hands are bound.
They appear in the sky. On one side is a black slave and on the other a Caribbean woman. They are the victims of Christopher Columbus who have bound the hands of God and prevented him from showing mercy.

The Mule kneels

6. What a tragedy! What is to be done!
Here's an idea! Let us get the Mule!*
The Mule is brought. She kneels.
The chains are broken. The hands of God are free!

Christopher Columbus delivered

The hands open slowly, and a dove flies out. It is the Holy Ghost coming to meet the soul of Christopher Columbus, also in the form of a dove.
Both fly to Paradise.

END

Paris, 9 March 1947

* The idea is: "O God, forgive the infinite stupidity of wretched humanity."
—P. C.

Alternative Beginning for the Film of Christophe Colomb

Scene i

1. All sorts of confused images drift over the screen. A torrent consisting of every imaginable mistake and absurdity (music in unison).
2. The director arrives in great agitation (wearing a morning coat with a flower in his buttonhole).
"What's going on?"
"We don't know. The film started off all by itself, and we can't stop it."
"*All right, I will fix that.*"[11] (He takes off his coat with the flower.)
3. Gradually the film sorts itself out and becomes clearer. But in all the scenes which I have indicated on the scenario, the director is there to impose discipline. He points his revolver at the gamblers to stop them from running away when Saint Hermandad comes to arrest them. He drags by the feet the man about to be hanged, and hands him over to the press gang. The executioner protests; he grabs hold of the executioner and hands him over with the others. He seizes a halberd and keeps the crowd in order. He walks backward in front of the column of recruits, beating time.
(All this in shirt sleeves and a bowler hat.)
March from *Aida*.
Etc.
4. In the final scene, while Christopher Columbus is rowing out to the ship, we see him in a very small boat going back to shore, mopping his brow.
Cannon shots as in the picture in the museum at The Hague.

Scene ii

1. The studio. The director, breathless and triumphant. He puts his coat on again, carefully adding the rose, which he had taken the precaution of sticking into a bottle before going out.
He parts his hair with a small comb and a pocket mirror
2. Tumult. Shrieks outside. What is going on?
3. It is Christopher Columbus' wife, and she is not pleased.
Curses the director. Traitor. Scoundrel. You sent my husband away, and what am I and my children going to do?

He's a coward, he's a madman. And here she goes through all Christopher Columbus' past history with Italian volubility.
4. The studio is deeply moved. The little script girl suddenly bursts into sobs. Also the cleaning woman with her broom. Everyone looks disapprovingly at the director. He tries in vain to clear himself of blame.
5. The director gnashes his teeth and tears his hair, trying in vain to make this Fury be quiet. Suddenly, look there! hush! Something is happening on the screen. . . .

And then, on the screen, the creation of the world and of America as in my scenario.

Scene iii

The Director:
1. And so you see, dear lady, I can do nothing. It's an act of God. Can't be helped. There's no way of stopping him. It isn't my fault.

Christopher Columbus has gone. We can only pray for his safe arrival and his return. Come, come—don't cry. It'll be all right. He gives her a sweet. All the staff crowd round Mrs. Christopher Columbus who is gradually consoled.

The Director:
2. Now we have to pray heaven for the success of Christopher Columbus. Let's go. Do you know who I'm going to fetch? Queen Isabella, no less. I know she likes Christopher Columbus. She ought to be in a good temper because she has just conquered the Moors.

The orchestra plays a little Moorish march.

Mrs. Christopher Columbus:
3. And I'm going to fetch Christopher Columbus' creditors. That's better still.

Business.

They go out.

From there on, as in the scenario, unless you have any suggestions.

22 April 1947

Partage de midi

From the letters to Jean-Louis Barrault, published in the complete
works of Claudel, we have selected those which refer fairly directly
to technical problems: sets, the *voice* in Mesa's hymn, and the arrangement of the final version, which we know to have been written
after the production:[12]

11, Boulevard Lannes, XVIe, 29 April 1948

My dear Barrault,
I had a talk yesterday with one of my successors at Foochow, Fernand
Pila, who has a good verascope photo of one of those magnificent
omega-shaped tombs at Foochow, about which I told you.
He also has some photos of the interior of Chinese temples.
It is all at your disposal whenever you wish.

Yours affectionately,
P. Claudel.

Brangues, 10 August 1948

MESA'S HYMN

I don't see any very serious difficulty here either. Why did I bring in
that *voice?* You know that at one time I studied Beethoven, and learnt
a lot from him from the point of view of composition. In him, as in
other musicians, there are two men, one who listens and one who
speaks. Music which listens and music which speaks. And in the same
way there is in every man someone who listens and someone who
speaks. The classical authors understood this perfectly. Rodrigue and
Polyeucte in their soliloquies do not speak; they listen to themselves. If

I had gone on writing plays, I would have made use of that idea, which strikes me as really dramatic. It's *true!* There are moments in life when we are forced to listen to someone talking. That was my idea—Mesa, beaten, broken and humiliated, listens. Unknown, repressed, and lonely, his turn comes at last.

But you are free to do as you like.

I agree with you entirely about the set dissolving and the sky filling the whole stage.

The music: I don't think we'll gain anything by bringing in ordinary music here; it is too precise, and would intrude too much and sound forced and artificial. But there is one thing you must have noticed. When you look with sufficient concentration at a wide starry sky, you perceive something—that the stars *make a noise.* What I mean is a teeming inexhaustible activity, with sudden spurts and diminuendos due not to a decrease of energy but to an increase of intensity. Something like a swarm of bees clinging to its chosen branch, but much more various, pulsating, bespangled. *Something that boils.*

The noise of the stars! Don't you think that would be something to inspire our friend Honegger? A few bars would be enough—perhaps coming back at the very end. A kind of sparkling chaos!

FINALE

You were absolutely right not to accept my last version. I wasn't satisfied with it myself. It was a step in the right direction. Now I think I'm there. At the very moment when I was going back to this obscure play, circumstances once more compelled me to appraise anew its meaning and contents and to work out the ending. It is quite different from that of the first version and not exactly the same as that of the second. But it seems to me the only possible one—as in *Le S. de satin*—being both obvious and simple. The audience must go away not worried but satisfied, and the ending of a play like this must be *simple,* complete, and sublime, all at once. I believe that is what I have at last managed to do.

Instead of the noisy meaningless lyricism of which I was capable in the first version—I really can and always could distinguish something that goes deep from something that merely scratches the surface—I've written this with my blood. I can sum it up in five words: logic, simplicity, *sweetness,* intensity, mystery.

And, in addition, I've thought of something in the set which will save a lot of words.

18 August 1948

My dear Barrault,

I've just received your letter of 16 August.

About the hymn—I'm sure we won't have any difficulty in coming to an agreement. If we try it out on the stage, that will decide it. Personally, I still believe in an exchange of views between the *two* Mesas and the "heavenly kettle" as you call it!

I can't give up hope of seeing you and Feuillère at Brangues. The play you forced on me (providentially, I am sure) has become enormously important to me. Hardly a day has passed when I haven't thought about it. Its performance will have an importance which I dare call "historic" —comparable with that of the *Soulier de satin*. It's a great work. It is an attempt to understand the meaning of my whole life. It's far more than literature.

For the *noise of the stars*, there are two possible comparisons:

1. The swarm. Relatively slow noise, which grows less as intensity and movement accelerate.

2. This beautiful sight—the dance of the atoms, tiny specks in a shaft of sunlight. In the middle of this kind of innumerable meditation, one of them suddenly does a sort of rapid arabesque and disappears.

3 December 1948

Dear. J.-L. B.,

I hope you'll manage to find that big armchair somewhere. At one time there was a shop specializing in Chinese furniture in the Rue du 4 Septembre. In any case there is no lack of models, and there would be time to make some attempt at concocting something *red.*

I'm worried about the gap before Ysé gets on to the "nuptial throne." I hadn't the script with me. If I were in Paris I would work that out for you in a few minutes.

The *hymn* has still to be sorted out. I think the idea of *muttering* is not at all bad. You were giving the impression of a dialogue so marvelously that you ought to have someone to talk to.

I think the idea of the omega contracting through the three acts until it becomes the size of this *nuptial throne* which encompasses both of them is not bad.

27 December 1948

I have listened with great delight to the two first acts of P. It's perfect now. You're completely on top of your part—and of the audience. It was remarkable how attentively they listened to the religious side of Mesa.

What hasn't improved is the props! That pair of tongs instead of a bell! I shall have to go round to the Canal S. Martin and get you the real thing, used on all the barges! And that indescribable siren!!

The whole thing done at full speed without any of the pauses which make it possible to bring into a play that essential element:

TIMING

3 January 1949

Dear friend,

Don't you think that at the end of Act III Ysé ought to put her candle back in front of the Virgin of Ciz—since she stops for a minute in front of M—and Am. comes and grasps her by the wrist and drags her away. People mustn't think they're going to the wedding arm in arm!

11, boulevard Lannes, XVIe

8 February 1949

My dear Barrault,

You know what trouble you had to persuade me to let *Partage de midi* be staged. I resisted, not only for personal reasons, but because I was aware that my work was imperfect—as the 1905 version bears witness. When I finally consented, I made some important alterations which paved the way to production and helped you and Edwige Feuillère to this magnificent success.

These alterations were not enough. Life is what matters, and a dramatic work does not really come to life until it reaches the stage. At Marigny for the first time I saw the thing from outside, separated from myself. From the second part of the second act onward, thanks to you and perhaps in spite of you, I felt the two actors in the Parable giving orders which became more and more pressing, and to which I finally had to yield. None of the plans I submitted to you, and with which you had to manage as best you could, had their final approval. It was absolutely necessary for them to get rid of all the lyrical fripperies which were strangling them, and which were quite unsuitable for the severities of passion.

But I can be sure of my art only with my pen in my hand. So I forced myself to recopy *Le Partage*, slowly and from beginning to end. I'm sending you the result of this work, and I have altered only what I thought really necessary and inevitable, inspired, and indispensable. I had you and Edwige constantly before my eyes, and the timbre of your voices in my ears. Nothing in it stems from caprice or ostentation; it all comes from humble obedience to an inner voice—in fact, to that deep sacred thing, the *heart*. The heart alone. It is the heart which, in the last scene, when destruction is about to overtake the body, Ysé brings at last to her lover, who is the mind. And it all ends with that raised hand, one single hand for both of them, that lonely, luminous hand, praying, commanding and calling—calling to another in the stars!

On Partage de midi

So this play, *Partage de midi*—which is not a creation of the spirit, but which happened, and for twenty years has dominated my whole existence—has at last been staged at your request, after more than twenty years! I have just seen it, and you want my impressions. In 1905, when I wrote the first version which of necessity remained unpublished for so long, I was only trying to give expression to my feelings in what language I had at the time. In 1948, when this sketch had to be translated into reality, the question for me was not only to take advantage of the surer touch which forty years' practical experience are bound to give an artist, but to see how the work would stand up to that *regard ennemi* of which Mallarmé speaks—the detached appraisal of the author after a long interval. The time had come to find out whether the anecdote could claim the dignity of a parable, whether it could move from the domain of sentiment to that of meaning.

I don't turn out work like a factory. I believe in inspiration. An inspiration over which I have no control and which chooses its own moment, not mine. All I have to do is to keep my mind free and watchful.

You haven't forgotten, Jean-Louis, the friendly arguments we had during the very last rehearsals. There was a crack somewhere, and I myself thought it was in the middle of the second act. And as for the third, we were neither of us satisfied with the ending, though it was much better than the 1905 one.

So then I gave you two or three suggestions. None of them was completely satisfying and each had its good points. And then we reached a compromise—the present version, which was not entirely unworthy of public acclaim.

But then an event occurred which was all-important to me. The play was performed. I saw Edwige Feuillère in the first act as produced by you. Everything was clarified and fell into place for me, and the play reached its final balancing point. Rather late!

It was a resurrection! Yes, this was the woman I had met—only yesterday!—on the deck of the *Ernest Simons*. No, I hadn't met her, I was part of the boat which she took over in one moment with an authority leaving no room for argument. It was the same dress, the same voice, the graceful swaying walk. Straight away she became the focal point. When she emerges from the companionway, her arms full of her variegated loot, she is distributing, not cushions, but parts in a play, with a peal of laughter which shakes you to the core. I watch fascinated. Yes, that is how it should be. Between a man and a woman on the stage there are, to use a sporting term, *holds* of every kind. But here, from beginning to end of the act, until eight bells are heard and the siren flings its despairing howl into the boundless solitude, Ysé keeps three men in subjection with a firm, graceful hand. Present or absent, she does not let them go for a second, until she has taken from them all that the play demands. With her voice, her glance, her hand, and, if need be, her long goddess-like walk, she has taken over command of the chessboard, and the human pawns depend on her alone. Until the tangle at the end, which Barrault has imagined so well, when, with Amalric officiating, cups are distributed in which a few drops of the elixir of legend may well lurk. Midday.

Second act. Hong Kong. The Happy Valley cemetery.

The magnificent Chinese tomb, the photo of which I provided, is still there, but alas! what has happened to the bamboo curtain behind it, which is so necessary? What can be more alive than a tomb? This one is only a lifeless imitation now, an empty shell, coming from nowhere. Huge though it is, it does not fill the stage. And what about that atmosphere of oppression and eclipse which I had purposely indicated in the script?

However, all goes well until page 148 of the script. From page 148 onward I think I can allow myself some ideas of my own.

There is no question of leaving the actors to their own devices, even though feeling and inspiration can be, and in fact are expected. But art needs a strictly logical approach, nowhere more necessary that in a scene of passion, and in the theatre to put something together means taking it apart. So let us take apart all the important moments in the scene between the lovers in Act II, which is the climax of the whole play.

First there is the moment when M., who is man, tremblingly takes possession of Y, who is woman. Barrault remembered the hundred-fingered hands of Nijinsky when, as the negro at the feet of Scheherazade, without even touching his partner, he enveloped her from head to feet in the warm wondering movement of those greedy antennae. The embrace follows. M. enters behind, and they speak in turn, without looking at each other. Nevertheless, it is time for each to take full account of the other (p. 141). I imagine that Y takes M by the hands and turns him round, to look at him and to show herself in every possible light (as in children's games, when the blindfolded one is turned round and round until he no longer knows where he is).

But not for one moment, right up to the end of the play, must Y's hold on her partner slip. At all costs this must not be allowed to crack (see line 7 on page 149 which was retained from the 1905 version). I cannot possibly imagine Ysé going and sitting down somewhere and uttering the big speech, the essential one, on pages 148–149 *into a vacuum*.

On the contrary, I see her face to face with her prey, holding him by both wrists. To bring out the idea of chains and of twisting, I see the four hands interlaced. And then two opposing movements. In the first, she draws him toward her (up to the end of 148). In the second (149) it is she who advances upon him step by step, in a progression measured by the words:

Donnés	*jetés*	*arrachés*	*lacérés*	*consumés*	This is the very
. . . .		*qui est l'éternité*			heart of the play.
Toucher			pause		
Prendre			pause (not too long)		
La mienne, etc. (Spoken very close to him, the syllables clearly detached, the accent on *sable*.)					

Then comes Act 4. Y. feels that in spite of everything there is something recalcitrant and insurmountable in M. An oath! That is what is needed! And then she has the idea of the sacrilegious oath before the cross (it should have been something more serious than those bits of wood). Her raised right arm is going to become important in Act III.

The rest is all right.

(These moments of extreme tension cannot be kept up for too long. Something must be sacrificed. But that can't be helped.)

Act III

The refuge in the pagoda. A good set, but too much furniture. The stage is too cluttered, which spoils the final effect. I would get rid of it all, and leave only a large red Chinese seat in which two people can sit at once (still the omega shape). I am thinking about those Etruscan funerary thrones on which husband and wife sit stiffly side by side. There was a picture of one of these in Duruy's *Histoire romaine* which made a great impression on me.

All goes well as far as what used to be the *Cantique de mesa*. I had to sacrifice that. I could no longer stand those great operatic airs like *L'Invocation à la nature* by Berlioz. I substituted a dialogue. In my long night journeys, I noticed that amid the host of slanting signals the stars were speaking. I had only to listen. Can it be denied that M's circumstances are perfect for that? There is something intimate and confidential about them. Mesa has already lost a skin. Now or never is the moment for explanations.

Thereupon Ysé reenters. Ah, my good fellow, did you really think you were going to get rid of her as easily as that? The woman's back already. "I forgive you," she says.

Partage de midi is a drama of passion. The characters prepare for passion, they receive it into their hearts, and it reaches its natural conclusion, which is suffering. No, not only suffering. Death? Not only death.

Oh, that 1905 version! The poet of 1905 knew all this, confusedly! Watch him floundering! Nevertheless, the stars are there.

The adventuress—the woman who risks and is at risk—of Act I is not the lover of Act II, who is not the wife of Act III. They are three different women. Three different atmospheres.

How well they know each other now, how well they understand each other, now that death is at hand and they are both ready to die together! How they burned for each other! how they needed each other! how they knew and how they hated each other! Hated because they knew each other through and through, and because of the inexorable fate which each brought to the other. The hook slipped on the stone and a swift current carried the boat away. And I could almost laugh to think that now we can never escape each other. That is the way it is.

I brought you your name which you did not know. And you—have you nothing to give me in exchange? The sky for example—that starry sky we can see through a hole in the roof. You have only to take it. Raise your hand!

And in fact, in the vast dark cavity of the theatre nothing is seen but that luminous hand, stretched . . . toward the sky . . . lit by a moonbeam.

On these words the play ends. The curtain falls, as the script says "like a thunderbolt."

L'Annonce faite à Marie

In 1944, the Compagnie du Regain toured *L'Annonce faite à Marie*. Claudel attended a performance at Lyons on May 12, and made a few notes on it.[13] Some of these dealt with very precise details, and others were general suggestions for the production. Claudel was particularly interested in the set:

PROLOGUE

Set. Passable. But I need a real door. We can do without St. Peter and St. Paul. When the door opens, I need light and a glimpse of green and blue.

ACT I

Courtyard side. I want a large fireplace in front of which the mother sits. . . .
I want a proper door which will open. Anne Vercors opens both sides when the oriole sings.

ACT II

Sets. It is absolutely essential for the three scenes to follow each other without any sort of interruption. To this end I suggest the following device, following the example of the *S. de Satin:*
The stage is divided into two parts. One-third of it represents the hall at Combernon, and two-thirds the garden. Each part has a separate curtain to be raised and lowered as needed.
The special set for the Adoue Fountain will have to be abandoned.

ACT III

This act has suffered most, and the most radical changes are needed here.

I am fairly satisfied with the first of the two sets and not at all with the second, which is completely inadmissable.

It is essential for the two scenes to follow each other without *any* break.

On several occasions in the past it was considered enough to indicate the forest by means of a series of strips of material (green, white, and black) in perspective, dropped from the flies. This device seems best to me. . . .

After scene 1, the Leper crosses the whole width of the stage, a clapper in her hand. It is almost completely dark (perhaps a moonbeam upstage). Only the sound of the clapper is heard, and we see only the almost indistinguishable forms of the two women. Then a red light comes on, right, in front of the Leper's cell, which is disclosed by several strips being raised.

The rocks seem decidedly to be condemned to give the worst result. I prefer a little cell with the four-centered arch of the lintel giving the effect of the period. Above, a little barred window: a door, an opening —a real opening, as this recess is to be used.

To the right of the door, a tall statue of the Virgin with a Gothic canopy indicated in long thin lines. At the foot, a red lamp is lit. The fire is not shown.

Stage left, a heap of rocks brought in while the stage is in darkness.

Costumes. Violaine's in *whitish* gray. *Very important.*

The child must never be seen, simply suggested under a voluminous shawl. . . .

"L'ANNONCE FAITE À MARIE"

Setting for Act II.

The stage is divided horizontally into two levels, A and B.

C. Transparent curtain strewn with flowers and leaves, pink and green.

D. Recess with the fireplace in front of which the Mother sits.

E. Steps.

In front of D a curtain which can be raised and lowered.

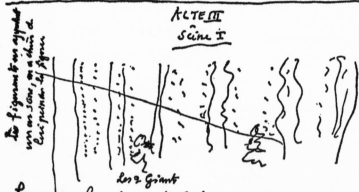

ACT III

Scene i

X. The two giants. The crowd brings one on to the stage and finishes painting its face.

Long strips of transparent material in green, white, purple, and deep violet in imitation of trees. Other strips behind, in depth. Diagonal spot.

Acte III

On a gardé les bandes q. représentent la forêt
Aussi le confournot de l'Act II. C'est main-
tenant la logette de la Lépreuse: Un peu à gauche.
Au fond elle s'assoit, vaguement éclairé par un feu
très faible. À droite un monticule sur lequel elle peut monter
À gauche une statue de pierre très longue et mince avec Baldy.
qui un gothique représentant la Vierge avec l'Enfant. À ses pieds
un pupitre, avec le livre recouvert d'une étoffe. Au dessus
une lampe. Devant la logette un banc où s'assoit V

A - monticule
B. - statue
C. Logette
D. Bandes arbres

À la fin éclairage
rose peu en haut

Scene iii

The strips of material remain, representing the forest.

Also the recess from Act II, which is now the Leper's cell. A little to the left. She sits in the background, very dimly lit. On the right a heap of stones on which she can climb. On the left a very long thin stone statue with a Gothic canopy, representing the Virgin and Child. At its feet a lectern with the book covered with material. Above, a lamp. In front of the cell a bench on which Violaine sits.

A. Pile of stones. C. Cell   At the end,
B. Statue   D. Strips forming trees   pink lighting from above

Shortly afterward, on 7 November 1944, Claudel wrote to Jean-Louis Barrault about the same play:

Finally, as far as the sets are concerned, I think we ought to abandon the decorative aspect in favor of the dramatic. The props for example—a door, a table, a staircase, a fireplace, or a lamp are fascinating characters, and at the same time they are the instruments of the action. What point is there in camouflaging them? Should we not rather bring out their functions by reducing them to a starkly general character? . . . More or less the same thing applies to the costumes. It is much less a question of painting a picture than of marking out a site.

> When, in 1948, the play in its final version was performed at the Théâtre Hebertot, Pierre Mazars reviewed it thus in the *Figaro Littéraire:*

This new production of L'Annonce *has a history. One day, while leafing through an American magazine, a girl belonging to the Claudel family exclaimed: "But that's the set of* L'Annonce!"

The picture in the magazine showed a huge building "with square pillars supporting ogival arches." It was an English manorhouse, Stocksey Hall, dating from 1240 and miraculously intact.

Paul Claudel saw the photograph with a violent shock and a sensation of "déjà vu." The interior he was looking at was the very one which he had himself created for the play from his imagination.

> The following article appeared in *Le Figaro* for 11 March 1948:

Some Ideas on Production

Those enthusiasts who kept the programmes of the first performance of *L'Annonce faite à Marie* at the Salle Malakoff on December 20, 1912, will find in it certain notes on the production which I wrote at Lugné-Poe's request. Though my ideas were in those days uncertain and confused, long experience has not proved them wrong. And M. Hébertot has had sufficient confidence in me to allow me to apply those same ideas to the staging of *L'Annonce*, working with an excellent collaborator, M. Vernier, and a team of actors as devoted as they are understanding.

(And the same faith, liveliness, and enthusiasm in old and young alike!)

The production of a dramatic work relates both to the spoken word and to the vicissitudes of the underlying action.

I have often had occasion to express my views on the verse form which seems to me better adapted to the needs of drama than alexandrine verse. The idea is borrowed from classical antiquity, and based on the *iambus* (a long syllable followed by a short). The actor must also take into account certain essential elements such as the interrelation of timbres (instead of rhyme) and the all-importance of consonants. (Not to mention the "head voice" for which actors, through bad teaching, tend increasingly to substitute a horrible and exhausting guttural shout. They imagine they are gaining force by yelling, but they would get it much more easily by clearly detaching their syllables.)

As for the ordering of the action, or production strictly speaking, it is so important, and calls for such intelligence, imagination, and ingenuity on the part of the person who does it, that I can only compare it with creation itself. I will mention here only one of the discoveries I have made in the course of the fascinating work of these last few weeks. It is that the production must have a "line." It is not a matter of accompanying the delivery of the words with more or less appropriate gestures and moves, in a random, slapdash sort of way. The actor must always feel supported, held fast, never left to himself, surrounded by uncertainty, stagnation, and emptiness. He is always coming from somewhere and going somewhere else with his whole being. It is like Anne Vercors going to Jerusalem. There are hands which push and hands which pull, and other hands on each side stretching out toward them. He is drawn irresistibly along a certain path, and not one of his movements is irrelevant.

> Claudel was wrestling with the same problems when the play was put on at the Comédie-Française in 1955.

I only want to stress one point, the correctness of intonation, which comes so rarely to delight an author's ear! You talk of music, but how weak and clumsy it is compared with poetry! Not strings or brass, but the soul itself is the instrument, and oh, the joy when, sometimes in conditions of infinite complication, the note is *right*. *Right*—and what beauty there is in that one word!

The Theatre in
the Process of Birth

In 1953 Jean-Louis Barrault produced *Le Livre de Christophe Colomb.* He recalls it as follows:

Claudel was also delighted to see his wish for the theatre in the process of birth *becoming reality on the stage.*

The company of actors was for him so much clay which my hands shaped into the story of Christopher Columbus.

In another article especially devoted to this production he speaks of actors, or actors and chorus alternately, using "the improvised means they have at their disposal." At least this would be the ideal type of production.

This was in fact an old dream of Claudel's; he tried to make it reality in his revival of *Tête d'or* in 1949:

The play gave me a chance to carry out an idea with which I had been toying for a long time, and which I tried to apply in my *Fourberies de Scapin.* A play in the process of birth. A play being born in front of the audience.

In this unfinished revival, the inmates of a German prisoner of war camp decide to put on *Tête d'or;* the production was to take shape gradually on the stage.

LE RAVISSEMENT DE SCAPIN
Preface

Bound hands making the sign of the Cross—that was the vision which led to the writing of Jeanne au bûcher. *Another vision, a little later, was—what do you think? A floating rope. A rope? I beg your pardon! We are in the theatre, and we may not mention that invisible, sacred cord which sets us brilliantly competing with reality. A floating rope. It floats among those cheerful taverns which you still find in the country—they were all like that in the seventeenth century. With a hook at the end, you can use it for storing in the loft those good things from the classics which our University is always discovering.*

Me too.

Molière for example. I shall never forgive him Le Misanthrope, *any more than I can forgive Corneille for* Polyeucte. *But what a lyric poet! There is another kind of lyricism besides the verbal one; it takes its elements from reality and translates them into wit. All at once the event has lost its seriousness, its barbs, its threat to our ego. The whole of life is reduced to situations. What wonderful use we can make of that as soon as we are detached from the drama and can look at it with the joyous eye of a man whom Bacchus has raised to a state of cheerfulness far superior to mere equilibrium! You talk of types: the Miser, the Hypocrite. . . . What do we care for types? They just set fire to each other! Avarice, money, love, pride, disease—what else is there?—death? Yes, that's it—death! It's a scream! Don't worry—go on, friend! Laurent only exists through the reply he extorts from Anastasie and both through their good fortune against Barbe and Saturnin! No need for an author—we are the author! Something is going to happen, and it matters to us what it is! Every word they say, do you hear? up there on the stage, we have whispered to them. And who has given us every word they say, up there on the stage?*

That is exactly what I have tried to show in the little play you are going to see. We have plenty of actors to draw on; they are in the pub, doing one thing and another—drinking, smoking, yawning, arguing, playing cards. . . . And suddenly someone brings on a large skip full of costumes and wigs. It's like an electric shock! Each immediately decides on his part. The play is taking shape all by itself before our eyes! For there is this rope hanging, that bag doing nothing in a corner, this hook ending discreetly in a trapdoor in the ceiling. . . . Come on then! Let's go!

And how delightful it is to collaborate with Molière, to repeat slowly, easily, passing one's tongue over one's lips, that prose in which everything is essential, nothing superfluous! No padding here, as there is in the greatest writers, Racine for example. No dead wood! It's vivid, muscular, it's all fire, elegance, vivacity, wholesome gaiety, strength! It would be wonderful to write like that.

The Announcer's part is taken by a cornet which gives a brilliant lecture on the laws and privileges of Comedy.

The audience, represented by various instruments of the orchestra, expresses its sentiments (remarks, applause, doubts, objections, scraps of discussion).

The curtain rises, and behind it is a transparent curtain behind which a confused hubbub can be heard.

A street seller chants: "Green and tender, green and tender!"

A curtain disappears.

A large room in a tavern, full of tables at which a large number of men and a few women are seated. Smoke-laden atmosphere. At one table people are playing dice, at another they are playing mora. The loser has his nose blackened with the help of a cork and a candle.

It is a tavern near the Théâtre-Français frequented mainly by actors.

When the curtain rises a group of men, directed by the innkeeper, are laboriously hoisting a barrel toward a trapdoor in the ceiling.

There is a blind man with his dog, playing a hurdy-gurdy very softly.

Two doors opening into lighted passages. One leads to the scullery. The other . . . exactly!

Enter two boys of fifteen to sixteen carrying a large wicker basket on their shoulders.

This basket of costumes makes actors of everyone in the tavern. They distribute costumes and wigs and begin playing, or rather playing with, *Les Fourberies de Scapin.*

The show takes shape before our eyes, not without discussion or argument.

A BROADCAST "EXTRAVAGANZA"

The same effect, less directly theatrical, is aimed at in this passage of the same period, from a revival of *L'Endormie, La Lune à la recherche d'elle-même:*

CHORUS: Let me explain! No writer ever reaches the end of his career without leaving behind him, if not always corpses, at least remorse. For example, the fragments of plays, limbs living, moving and quivering, which have never managed to become part of a body. And landscapes too, paragraphs on nature and the passing moment which the poet has never succeeded in explaining satisfactorily to anyone. A night with a full moon, for example, in a landscape of fields and forests; you have only to shut your eyes and you will see as I do the stillness of a Creation which, now that everyone is asleep, is given over to the magic of solitude. How often those whose task it is to listen to the voice of the mind have tried to do justice to it—with varying degrees of success. The particular charm of a night lit by a full moon is not only the impression of immense peace, of a general holiday, which is perhaps a desire not to disturb our satellite in its journey from one horizon to the other of the map spread for it in our dreams. The everyday and familiar, not to say trivial world to which we are accustomed in the daytime has become something solemn and sacred. The poet realizes that it is not a question of painting it, but rather of dreaming it. But here is the amazing contradiction—what do we derive from this ecstasy, this fascinated silence? A kind of religious fury, a mad longing for violence, a need to howl and stampede! It must be so, since classical literature is full of the procession of Cybele and the exploits of Bacchus and the Corybantes; and if you don't believe me, I know somebody who is stuffed with Latin and Greek sesquipedaliantics. How can all this be reconciled? It's torture for the author, and in despair he has decided today to fall back on me, such as I am. For I, you see, am the Chorus. In other words, I am deputizing for a freighter who is not too sure of his cargo and has asked me to accompany him like the good friends who walk along beside poor people's carts so as to be there to give a hand with the furniture. And if you don't mind, I'm going to have a drink. Good health!

THE MAN IN CHARGE OF STAGE DIRECTIONS: He has a drink.

CHORUS: Just imagine—the author in question, having reached an age when he would have every right to think himself firmly set in his ways, has suddenly become fourteen again! I mean that a fiendish mistress—I think it was the Moon herself—has put back into his hands a monster he was guilty of creating at that age of innocence and which, after sixty years or more, has still not managed to get itself born? As you can imagine, a schoolboy cannot help peopling the immense Moon with schoolmasters—I mean with fauns and nymphs and anything else he can grab from the classics. They are there for a child to turn on like a tap. And why not fauns and nymphs as well as anything else? Demibeasts and demigods, lashing hooves, living explosions, goats' ears and kangaroos' legs with little feet scarcely touching the ground—those are the kind of characters you want. Listen, then. I'm fourteen, and I'm as curious as you are—as impatient, even—to know how I am going to begin my little tale. The first thing to do is obviously to create the atmosphere as they say. If I were a musician, it would be easier. The simplest course would be to put the record at the disposal of this pickup which is all ready and waiting for the good things in store for it.

THE MAN IN CHARGE . . .: He puts on the record. The machine starts to bellow at the top of its voice: *Marguerite elle est malade.* . . . He manages to stop it.

CHORUS: You will ask what that Bacchic refrain is doing here. But put yourselves in the place of that little boy at the highest window of an old castle, every hair on his body standing on end, his soul, his eyes, his heart, everything, filled with that ocean of ecstasy I am trying to describe to you, those mountains, forests, cornfields, and vineyards spread out below him; and in a corner somewhere is that almost invisible little orchestra with its big drum and its cymbals and the raucous brass coming back again and again—enough to make you sob to yourself. Ah, how you long to fling yourself into that awesome chaos and swim across it with shouts of frenzy! For our thinker is not taken in by that riot of glory which he has to follow all through every hour of this splendid month. He knows that Selene up there has also been called Hecate! He remembers certain nights at the equinox, and that yellow horse among the clamorous Valkyries, galloping across a tattered sky! And then below, on the stretched canvas of mystery, something is seen on all sides, something flashing and brooding at the same time, leaping in sudden pools of light. All God's creation is caught up in the challenge of midnight—why then should we not imagine passing through it, something which is a woman, and a hind, and the sow of Erymanthus, an immense drunken hussy, a sort of human avalanche, constantly crying out and replying as it slides with mad momentum down the slippery slope of a volcano!

THE MAN IN CHARGE . . .: Noise of a motorcycle in the distance.

CHORUS: But now, *sufficit.* I hear the sound of a motorcycle down in the forest, which is going to deprive you of my company. But first let me put at your disposal the whole of the sparkling black landscape from which you are separated by an impassable veil, and sow it with fauns and nymphs—according to the wish of the old scribbler whose enterprise I am asked to support today—and that is all the easier for me, since fauns and nymphs—oh yes, you shall have your fauns and nymphs!—are really only voices these days. Do you hear? They are on every side—eyes listening and ears speaking, under the grass, under the branches . . . Wait a minute! There's one just there, on the slender tip of the tall poplar above our heads. . . .

Last Words on the Theatre

DRAMA

The epic poem is a spectacle, the dramatic poem is an action. An action carried out by actors. As the epic poem develops a situation, that is to say a kind of moral setting; drama gives concrete form to one of those unformulated, more or less meaningful controversies among which our daily life moves continually. It completes it, authenticates it, raises it to the status of an example. The atmosphere, and the resulting general tone, are not the same as those of the epic. The storyteller remains consciously quite apart from his story. But with drama we penetrate into the darkest region of the human brain, that of dreams. In dreams our mind is reduced to a passive or semipassive state, called the *plateau*, and invaded by ghosts—and where do they come from? not only from the memory—which induce us to take part in bringing an event to pass. I call drama a guided dream. Once the theme, wherever it may come from, is settled, the characters come into being, recruited by a masked impresario, and work it out from exposition to coda. Gradually all becomes organized. Not like real theatres (if you can call them that . . .) where you pay for your seat, and there are only inarticulate attempts at communication between auditorium and stage. Here there is a physical attraction between the two, as between the mother and the embryo. The initiative comes from the stage, but what a chorus the audience makes! Let us not speak of the critics, pitiless as they are! Let us not speak of the two producers, one right, the other left, on the prompt side and opposite the prompter, explaining to the actors, as the play goes on, who they are and what they have to do. Let us speak of those same actors stamping furiously in the wings in their eagerness to get into their parts. Let us speak of the clamorous torrent of words which little by little forces on with gathering speed a plot which creates its own laws and its own verisimilitudes, so that its expression literally gushes out beneath our feet! Let us speak of the audience in tears, greedily waiting to know the end. One voice was not enough for the poet; he had to have that group working together on the stage. And that multitude, hungry for truth and for the Absolute behind the daily illusion, needs the kind of sacrifice that takes place on that wooden eminence![14]

THE PLEASURES OF THE THEATRE

There are various elements in the pleasure felt by the audience at a play. First there is the pleasure of logic, of a plot constructed within the bounds of probability. In life, nothing happens strictly in order; on the whole we see only mutilated, abortive, imperfect actions, whereas drama shows us events depending on a more or less strict logic, and reaching a conclusion which is pleasing to God, since its underlying principle is order. That is one of the elements of the pleasure we find in drama.

Secondly, there is a pleasure rather like that of painting. Painting gives pleasure through the juxtaposition of colors, as music does by that of timbres . . . at least that is one of the elements of music. Similarly, in the theatre we derive pleasure from the juxtaposition of the characters and the different reactions they provoke in each other. It is interesting, for example, to see the effect of the different characters of *Hamlet* on each other. Even apart from absolutely strict mechanical logic, there is a harmony to be found in the relationships of the characters as such, reacting one upon the other as yellow can react on blue and red on green, but with infinitely more detail, because it does not appeal to only one of our senses, sight. It speaks also to our understanding and to our heart.

And that word "heart" leads me to a third reason, a third reply, because our heart too craves satisfaction. In daily life it finds continual opportunities to be active, but very rarely to be completely so. But a great poet, by creating a fictitious plot, gives the heart the chance to act and to express itself (the two most important things) in full.

Music speaks only to the senses. Poetry calls into being all forms of intelligence, character, feeling, and speech. Because speech also is capable of giving joy.

That is the element of delight I was telling you about. This delight arises not only from the appeal to our feelings, which have no chance to function in ordinary life, but from an enchanting synthesis of these different feelings, not only static, as in a piece of sculpture, but dynamic, moving logically—with a logic that is at least all its own—from beginning to end, not counting the complications and subplots it brings with it.

This is possible with an immense dramatic panorama; and it is possible in *Le Soulier de satin*, while an action confined to four characters, as in classical drama in general, and also in some of my plays, does not have room for those great waves which every intense, powerful action sets going around it.

For the first time *Le Soulier de satin* shows us these waves, stretching almost to infinity; and around an action between two characters—or three if you like—within narrow limits, we can see the development, the flowering, of a personal conflict, a personal contact between two beings. . . .

You said that the play was set in a kind of general situation within which it had to develop. I don't see it quite like that. In a play, the action itself creates the world around it. It does not unfold within a predetermined world. It cannot use a historical event as the Romantic writers did, as a setting for a picturesque plot. The drama itself, by its own intrinsic logic, creates, so to speak, the world around it, whether this world borrows elements from reality or is purely imaginary.

Having made this first observation, I'll answer your second question. You ask me whether I don't expect too great an effort on the audience's part. When *Le Soulier de satin* was being considered at the Théâtre-Français, it was debated whether the audience could be expected to listen for two and a half hours without interruption, which had never been done in France. And the director-general Vaudoyer said to me: "The audience will never stand that!" Especially as there was an enormous number of innovations in the style of the play, the development of the plot, and the production, it was thought that the audience would be confused and overwhelmed.

Nothing of the sort happened. I was amazed to see that the audience watched without any trace of boredom or displeasure, followed the play with perfect attention, and when the end of that very long act came, they even appeared to be demanding more. They did not show any signs of indigestion; in fact, they wanted only one thing—for the play to continue.

Success depends on the skill of the poet, of the producer—in fact, on a great number of things. But a logical, natural plot, playing on the audience's deepest feelings, can be prolonged much more than is done at present. . . .

The problem of audience participation naturally involves the actor, who plays an essential part. But there are two other elements. There is the intensity and power with which the poet translates into literary or poetic form the feelings and passions of the actors on the stage. This is the purely personal, I mean purely individual side. We see it at its strongest in that admirable play *Phèdre*, which is one of the masterpieces of the human mind. The beauty of the sentiments, the truth of the passions of each character, taken in isolation and together, obviously have an enormous hold on the public. That is the individual side.

But there is also what I call the constructive side—the composition of the play. The audience is interested in a character, not only for his own sake, but in view of his part in the action. If what the actor says answers the situation—what is called the situation from the dramatic point of view—and if the actors on the stage express themselves powerfully and credibly, I would go further: if necessary, the situation exactly as it is—say for example the situation in the first or second act of *Phèdre*—will give rise to a very intense degree of interest and participation which will plunge the audience right into the middle of the drama. . . .

Probability is a fringe product, and plays no essential part. Naturally, we must not do it too much violence, because then we become artificial, which is quite different. But when we have to come to the heart of a passion, we depend on certain historical or real circumstances. I do not think the matter is very important.

If you look very closely at *Oedipus Rex*, for example, you will see that it is based on a series of absolutely glaring improbabilities. Not one of the coups d'état, so to speak, of which *Oedipus Rex* consists, has anything whatever to do with probability. And yet the audience follows with beating heart the whole of this cock-and-bull story, at which the Athenians, if they had any critical spirit at all, must have turned up their noses just as much as the French.

But the important thing was that the action itself, that is to say the true subject of the action—the misfortune of a man persecuted by the gods through no fault of his own—was treated with perfect logic, though, as we must recognize, with scant regard to probabilities. This is the case in almost the whole of Greek drama. Even the story of

Phèdre is not a very likely one if we look at it closely; it is rather improbable, for example, that a monster should come along and remove Hippolytus. In order to bring the plot to a close, the author needs certain events, which he brings in as best he can. If they come in naturally, so much the better; if not, it isn't very important provided the author knows his job.[15]

HERNANI'S HORN

Why were the strongest emotions I have ever felt in the theatre in my life caused by two poets for whom my admiration has long been on the wane—Victor Hugo and Richard Wagner? I wonder who was right, the ironical, disillusioned old man I have become, or the ten-year-old boy sitting in the Théâtre-Français in an intoxicating flood of poetry, and seeing the abysses of fate and love yawning before him. Or, later, the mature man, newly shaken by a terrible crisis, listening to the star of purity triumphing over the despairing magic of the Venusberg. How well I remember! It was at a performance at the Volksoper in Vienna—not very good, I was told—of *Tannhäuser*, a work for which modern musicians have nothing but scorn. It was nevertheless enough to let loose within me a whirlwind of sobbing passion which stayed with me from the overture to the last chord of its heroic ending. The flesh cried out, and so did the soul, and the struggle together of these equal champions was the very expression of myself. That was what I needed! And how despicable the morbid abandon of *Tristan* seemed in comparison! There is a moment between harsh youth and the over-oxidization of age when the wines of Burgundy reach their full maturity. It is the same with the sounding brass of Wagner. How masculine, how beautiful are those deep stern calls to manhood! Even the echoes of *Rienzi* and its alien fanfares did not worry me. Far from it! And the effeminate dilettanti can purse their lips as much as they like!

And *Hernani!* I saw this during the Great Exhibition of 1878; my father had managed to get seats in the gods at the Théâtre-Français for himself and me. Mounet-Sully played the doubleted hero, and Sarah Bernhardt Doña Sol. Both were in their fresh and fervent youth. At the disastrous revival this year everyone laughed, and with good reason, at the absurd melodramatic *dénouement*, particularly the distant horn reminding the two lovers, swooning in a supreme embrace, of the rights of virtue and death. I was not slow to add my sneers to the general derision. But that night my conscience came to reproach me. Was he as wrong as all that, the ridiculous little boy lit by the sun of MacMahon between the towers of the Trocadéro? No, the heart is never wrong....[16]

THE CHINESE THEATRE

What you tell me reminds me of my admiration for the Chinese theatre. I was in contact with it for the first time at the Exhibition of 1889. At that time there were some Annamite actors whom Claude Debussy also admired very much. . . . And then when I was in China I went to the theatre a great deal. . . .[17]

SHAKESPEARE, AESCHYLUS, AND RACINE

I might say I learned English from Shakespeare. I began it with a dictionary in one hand and Shakespeare in the other, and I worked very hard and quite successfully. At that time I had a boundless admiration for Shakespeare—I still have, to some extent—which was a great help. When people see my first version of *Tête d'Or* they always notice Shakespeare's influence; the wealth of images, the movement, the method of composition, are all Shakespearian.

Then Shakespeare led me to the Greek tragedies, which I had already learned to admire in the Commentaries of Paul de Saint-Victor which I read at school. That is yet another of my past enthusiasms.

I began to read Aeschylus in the translation by Leconte de Lisle, which I thought horrible. . . .

I said to myself, it just isn't possible. Aeschylus can't be like this. So I decided I must read him in the original. But in order to read him in the original I had to start again with a large part of my school work; I realized, nevertheless, that this was indispensable, because Aeschylus was giving me the education in prosody which I needed. Epic verse and dramatic or lyric verse belong in my opinion to two different systems. You cannot use epic or alexandrine verse in drama; I think it is a complete mistake. The dramatic or lyric verse form *par excellence* is the iambic. All great dramatic poets have written iambic verse—the Greek tragic dramatists, Shakespeare, and the great lyric poets, Pindar, etc. All their verse is based on the iambus, that is to say a short syllable followed by a long one: tick-tock, tick-tock, or else tick-tick-tock, tick-tick-tock.

The alexandrine and the hexameter, on the other hand, are narrative forms, and it is absurd to apply them to drama, except in the case of geniuses like Racine who, I admit, uses them brilliantly. Racine is one of the most extraordinary exceptions in literature. . . .

While I am on the subject, I must say that I have not found in any language in the world, not in Shakespeare, not among the Greeks, nor anywhere, anything to equal the three great plays of Racine, *Britannicus*, *Phèdre*, and *Athalie*. I think they are masterpieces, but alien to me. It is possible to admire something even while feeling that it is completely outside your own sphere. I understand Racine, but as something entirely outside myself, which has nothing to give me personally. . . .

First let me say what appeals to me in Shakespeare. In spite of everything I count him in the first rank, among the four or five greatest writers existing. In some respects I put him even above Racine, although I am not sure I am right.

Shakespeare has first of all the universal quality of his ideas. His works are a world in themselves. He has this violent inspiration, this dramatic impetus, this imagination which is a mixture of the familiar and the sublime. All this moved me to the highest pitch, and perhaps at that time I was excited even by the works I like least, like the early historical plays or *Romeo and Juliet*, the language of which is in appallingly bad taste, like a string of grandiloquent gibberish. Yet it has such youth, violence of inspiration, and intrepidity of sentiment that it raised me, and still does, to the highest pitch of excitement. Shakespeare was, after all, a very great man.

And then, after the magnificent plays of his maturity, we come to those works that mark almost the highest achievement of the mind of man—Shakespeare's five last plays. They are astonishing works, reaching almost supernatural heights of poetry: *Cymbeline*, *A Winter's Tale*, *The Tempest*. . . . I believe there are five of these last works.

Shakespeare began with comedy, then drama, and finally reached a kind of beatific vision recalling that of Beethoven, which appears in his last works. It corresponds to a very special use of verse, based on enjambment. From *A Winter's Tale* onward Shakespeare no longer breaks his lines as inspiration dictates, but tears them apart so that they bleed. The breaks come in totally unexpected places.[18]

EURIPIDES AND SOPHOCLES

I have an immense admiration for both Sophocles and Euripides, particularly Euripides, who comes very close to Baudelaire in feeling. I find it difficult to put them even a very little below Aeschylus. They are very great men, both of them.[19]

CALDERON AND LOPE DE VEGA

I have had in my possession an anthology of Spanish plays, some by Calderon, some by Lope de Vega, but on the whole I skimmed through them without paying sufficient attention. Actually, I think that Lope de Vega and Calderon, much more than some really great dramatic poets, are absolutely marvelous at devising plots. They are good at inventing plays rather then at creating them fully. I can hardly think of them as great poets. But they are, as I said, manufacturers of absolutely wonderful dramatic machinery. The best proof of that is that a large part of our classical theatre owes its life to the "blueprints" they invented, showing an incredible wealth of imagination.[20]

Conversation on Jean Racine[21]

PAUL CLAUDEL: My dear Arcas, you must blame this sciatica which until yesterday, alas, prevented me from arranging this interview I was so anxious to have with you.

ARCAS: Why me?

PAUL CLAUDEL: Are you not the Confidant *par excellence?* The confidant of all the princes and heroes whom my compatriot from the Ourcq has chosen as his actors? Not counting the conversations which your important functions allow you with the female satellites of so many charming personalities?

ARCAS: That's true. If it were not for us, what would happen to all those dressed-up people on the other side of the footlights?

PAUL CLAUDEL: What a lot of time-wasting you save! How marvelously they economize on properties, thanks to you! A few lines from you, the time and the place, and we know all about it. All we have to do is to set down the champions in the arena, beak to beak and spurs at the ready, like a cockfight, impatient to match their strength.

ARCAS: To match their strength, you say? Careful! That phrase is going to take us a long way.

PAUL CLAUDEL: How unjust it is, Arcas, Acaste, Paulin and all the rest of you, to reproach you with being conventional because you are indispensable! On the contrary, it is an excellent idea to condense in one single character all the retorts and criticisms which we need to hear from outside ourselves if we are to be provoked into replying—to let me, so to speak, deck myself in my own echo! Musicians understand this; they realize that no theme can get far without its countermelody.

ARCAS: Indeed, the simplest way to make yourself understood is to explain yourself.

PAUL CLAUDEL: *Explain yourself*, that's the word! French is about the only language in which the same word means "explain yourself" and "have it out with somebody," and France is the only country with such a passion for "having things out." Here, a quarrel or a fight is called an "explanation!" A calling to account—by force of arms.

ARCAS: Your beloved Shakespeare, that very Shakespeare you have admired so much in the past, yes, well, all these Shakespearian types . . . there aren't any confidants in Shakespeare!

PAUL CLAUDEL: Yes, there are. There is at least one.

ARCAS: Who?

PAUL CLAUDEL: Yorick. You know, the skull Hamlet picks up and swings on the end of a shovel.

ARCAS: You're not taking this seriously.

PAUL CLAUDEL: And you're taking it far too seriously. Here's a colleague dug up for you, and you ought to appreciate him as I do.

ARCAS: I would rather hold Shakespeare's skull in my hands. I could ask him for some explanations.

PAUL CLAUDEL: Explanations again! Try to understand that you don't explain Shakespeare; it just happens. A play by W.S. is an entertainment served up to you. It isn't a drama, it's a string of events which you're invited to look at. The curtain falls to show you it's finished.

ARCAS: Racine, now, or even Corneille, that's different!

PAUL CLAUDEL: Of course. Something has been cleared up. They've sorted it out, explained themselves, as you would say. The quarrel has been settled, the argument has been settled. The stalls have had their money's worth, and they are happy.

ARCAS: Whereas *Macbeth*, for example! Just imagine, when you wakened me, I was sleeping, not on the shores of Aulis, but in your library, *cheek by jowl* (as they say)[22] with a copy of that masterpiece, which was sticking into my ribs and giving me nightmares.

PAUL CLAUDEL: As it happens, I wanted to talk to you about *Macbeth*. You'll see why in a moment. I respectfully ask your opinion of it.

ARCAS: The author himself gives you that near the end of his egregious effort:

> *It is a tale*
> *Told by an idiot, full of sound and fury,*
> *Signifying nothing.*

PAUL CLAUDEL: That wouldn't be a bad description of quite a number of masterpieces of the Elizabethan theatre. But you must realize, my dear Mr. Arcas, that you can't dismiss the great William as lightly as that.

ARCAS: Are you defending *Macbeth?*

PAUL CLAUDEL: What I admire above everything in that magnificent play is its unity.

ARCAS: You're joking, of course.

PAUL CLAUDEL: There are other unities besides those which leap to the eye.

ARCAS: And what do yours leap to?

PAUL CLAUDEL: You remember that at the blackest moment of this horrific drama, when Macbeth, urged on by his wife, is murdering the King of Scotland, a heavy, dense atmosphere reigns, like that in the second before an earthquake. Atmosphere! That's the word I was looking for! The unity of atmosphere! A sinister, ominous atmosphere that does not lift from beginning to end of the play. Where was I?

ARCAS: The King of Scotland was just having his throat cut.

PAUL CLAUDEL: At that moment—midnight!—terrible, thunderous blows are heard on the castle gate. The same completely inexplicable thing as once happened to me—do you remember?—in an old house in Avignon.

ARCAS: Bang, bang, bang! There is a similar effect in Aeschylus, when Orestes is demanding entry to the palace where his lady mother awaits him.

PAUL CLAUDEL: Dare I say that these battering-ram blows—which Victor Hugo heard almost every night in his haunted house in Guernsey —formed the theme around which Shakespeare constructed his whole play?

ARCAS: Come now, this is too much even for my professional patience!

PAUL CLAUDEL: I can well imagine Shakespeare being wakened like that in some gloomy inn in Northumberland. Besides, between ourselves I'm not sure that our friend always had a perfectly clear conscience. Racine himself . . .

ARCAS: What's this?

PAUL CLAUDEL: I read that at one point the guardians of law and order were not above giving him a long cool look.

ARCAS:

> *Oubliez-le, Seigneur, et qu'à tout l'avenir*
> *Un silence éternel cache ce souvenir.*[23]

PAUL CLAUDEL: With what art the terrified poet used this brutal intervention of Fate! You remember the drunken porter's dialogue with the dreadful unknown creature battering on the other side! And all this time, in the darkness, the King's warm blood is seeping, drop by drop, through the floor and dripping on the face of the honest sentinel snoring below. And in the last act, when Lady Macbeth, a candle in her hand, is wandering in her sleep around the inextricable maze of her crime, it is not the deed itself she recalls, but those terrible doom-laden blows. *To bed! to bed! there's knocking at the gate! Come, come, come, come, give me your hand; what's done cannot be undone. To bed, to bed, to bed!*

ARCAS: And you say that these blows, deep in that great resounding drum which is the poet's imagination, gathered together all the elements of the play, and still hold it suspended amid their dark vibrations?

PAUL CLAUDEL: That is what I say. And what good are your criticisms now? From beginning to end of the play the atmosphere is that of a dream. In dreams moral consciousness is paralyzed, barriers are down, events follow each other without logical sequence and with an ease which has nothing to do with probability. It's somnambulistic. You remember the dagger which floats before Macbeth's hallucinated eyes. He does not seize it; rather it chooses to hover within the grasp of his guilty hand. And then remorse becomes fear, and then panic; with the gathering speed so typical of dreams, it engenders fresh misdeeds, and gradually engulfs and ousts reality. The Underworld is not slow to spew forth its demons and ghosts. Lady Macbeth is the human soul deprived of that sacred light that shines on every man entering this world, and for which the smoky candle trembling in her hand is but a poor substitute. Night has fallen! She has lost her bearings, and no longer knows where she is.

ARCAS: This is all very primitive. But in Racine the atmosphere, as you call it, is often not as different as you think, and it becomes convincing in other ways. Remember the end of Andromaque. Or of Britannicus, or of Bajazet, or of Phèdre. That alexandrine couplet can be like a tolling bell, like the voice of Fate.

PAUL CLAUDEL: You can prefer your alexandrine couplet as much as you like! Some people prefer straight lines to all the frills in the world. We'll discuss that presently. Why are you groaning, my dear sir?

ARCAS: I was just trying to clear my head of the fumes of images and metaphors with which my neighbor in the library was suffocating me. There was one prinking in every line!

PAUL CLAUDEL: Atmosphere, my dear sir, atmosphere!

. . . .

PAUL CLAUDEL: *Et cetera!* That is the verse of a man of the theatre who can model or sketch a whole attitude in one movement, without the bow leaving the string nor the pencil the paper.

ARCAS: Ah, how delightful for an actor to hear himself stretched to the very limit of his powers!

PAUL CLAUDEL: But now it's time I explained to you why we spent so much time on *Macbeth*. And we're going to end our conversation with *Phèdre*.

ARCAS: It's quite a way from Dunsinane to Troezen.

PAUL CLAUDEL: It's the same atmosphere. Remember—
> *Arrachons-nous d'un lieu funeste et profané*
> *Où la vertu respire un air empoisonné.*[24]

ARCAS: Atmosphere again! *Phèdre* is an atmosphere all to itself.

PAUL CLAUDEL: You mustn't get annoyed.

ARCAS: Just as Racine is far above anything in the world you can compare him with, so *Phèdre* is far above Racine himself. That was one of those moments when a writer, poor fool that he is, learns what it is to be a man of genius.

PAUL CLAUDEL: I agree.

ARCAS, *declaims:*
> *Salamine témoin des pleurs de Péribée!*[25]

PAUL CLAUDEL: I can go on giving you cues all night.

ARCAS:
> *Ariane aux rochers contant ses injustices.*[26]

PAUL CLAUDEL: It is even said—
> *Qu'avec Pirithoüs aux Enfers descendu*
> *Il a vu le Cocyte et les rivages sombres,*
> *Et s'est montré vivant aux infernales ombres.*[27]

ARCAS: You think Racine went down to Hell? That must have singed his wig!

PAUL CLAUDEL: Not the Hell of *Macbeth*, of course! Not the Hell of the Edda—the one Ibsen made hot and cold again for us in that play of his, you know, *Little Eyolf*—but the real, ancient Hell, the Hell whose doors the Son of Man opened. Only from Hell, from the true Hell, could a play like *Phèdre* come.

ARCAS: There is no doubt of it. Phaedra is as much a Christian as you or I.

PAUL CLAUDEL: Hippolytus too is a Christian. There is a similar situation in Homer—a certain Phoenix who makes no bones about cuckolding his Dad. But for Phaedra, crime is not a threshold over which one steps unawares. What a sight it is—that doomed innocent in the grip of the ancient Fates! The exits are well-guarded—Venus on the left side and Neptune on the right side. And presently the Monster itself, Leviathan, the Monster of Job and of the Apocalypse, will unfurl in a hurricane of tentacles on the promontory dark with past history.

ARCAS: Can I get a word in?

PAUL CLAUDEL: Go on, then.

ARCAS: While you were talking I was leafing through my little yellow book. You remember what you were saying to me just now about that famous "nucleus of the human heart" and the way Racine chose to split it with the same burning passion for research as our modern atomic scientists. Now listen! Aricie is speaking.

> *Phèdre en vain s'honorait des soupirs de Thésée.*
> *Pour moi, je suis plus fière, et fuis la gloire aisée*
> *D'arracher un hommage à mille autres offert,*
> *Et d'entrer dans un coeur de toutes parts ouvert.*
> *Mais de faire fléchir un courage inflexible,*
> *De porter la douleur dans une âme insensible,*
> *D'enchaîner un captif de ses fers étonné,*
> *Contre un joug qui lui plaît vainement mutiné. . . .*[28]

what do you think of that?

PAUL CLAUDEL: I think it is quite wrong to assert that in *Phèdre* there is only one character, Phaedra, that all the passion is hers, and the others are only "extras." Jean-Louis Barrault put this masterpiece on to a new canvas, as has been done with certain Rembrandt paintings, and thanks to the way he has brought out the part of Oenone, the first act was, for me, one of the greatest revelations of my artistic life. And the same with Hippolytus. Under the cloak of paganism, I see in him a martyr for purity, like those great figures whose acquaintance I made long ago in Alban Butler's *Lives of the Saints*. It is so touching, his idyll with that other martyr, Aricie, in a poetic Elysium worthy of Virgil and

Dante. A cruel father comes to his son from Hell, bringing its night-mares with him. But saints are not afraid of the Devil. Hippolytus strikes at the monster and makes a great wound in its flank. And when Hippolytus dies, leaving his blood to the Pallantidae as the ransom for a kingdom usurped, a ray of liberation lights up the dark shadows of the ancient Fate against which the unhappy Phaedra protested.

ARCAS: I am glad to see you are interested in Hippolytus. By some strange whim, Racine allotted to him—as he did to several other young men—the difficult task of resisting a woman passionately in love.

PAUL CLAUDEL: I have been thinking about that momentous scene in Act II in which Phaedra declares her love, and I think it could be worked differently.

ARCAS:

> *Pour en développer l'embarras incertain?*[29]

PAUL CLAUDEL: There is a line in Scene VI, when Hippolytus is confiding in Theramenes, which was like a ray of light to me.

ARCAS: Which one?

PAUL CLAUDEL: *Je ne puis sans horreur me regarder moi-même.*[30] You understand? We too find it hard to look at this virtuous Joseph driven back against the wall by Potiphar's wife, burning as she is with all the fires of lust. But if we imagine rather a kind of connivance, an involuntary attraction. . . .

ARCAS: Against the wall? Or against the statue of Venus which must inevitably be there?

PAUL CLAUDEL: Suppose, as I say, it was the other way round? Suppose it was Phaedra moving backward, and Hippolytus, fascinated, not knowing what he was doing, coming slowly, slowly, step by step toward her . . .

ARCAS: And suddenly he realizes that terrible attraction beneath whose spell he is falling . . .

PAUL CLAUDEL: And then the tigress flings herself upon him . . .

ARCAS: To snatch his sword . . .

PAUL CLAUDEL: All right . . . to snatch his sword . . .

ARCAS: Not an easy business, with those property swords. They're not unlike the swords that the guardians of law and order on our boulevards used to have hanging at their sides not so very long ago.

PAUL CLAUDEL: Actually the sword is only a pretext. What that mad-woman wants is contact—an embrace, if only for a second. Body to body, as close as can be! The sword is only a pretext. We have come to the essential part of the play. The essential point, in fact, of all Racine's plays. This longed-for, impossible embrace, lasting but a second . . . What do you think of my idea?

ARCAS: It's worth trying—why not?

PAUL CLAUDEL: You feel as I do that the human drama is not complete until a superhuman element enters into it. The *Iliad* and Greek tragedy owe their greatness to this intervention of supernatural forces in our battles. They are there in *Macbeth*—I mean those of evil. And in *Phèdre* too, and again those of evil. Venus and Neptune, whom I see present in their archaic statue form from beginning to end of the five acts, are more than a match for Hecate and her witches. But what gives the drama its poignancy—because it is not only Phaedra's, but Racine's too—is the question it asks of the conscience of anyone who is inspired, who is both victim and accomplice of an unknown, ambivalent, and questionable power. At the very beginning of tragedy, on the very threshold of that terrible door from which so many masterpieces were to emerge, old Aeschylus set up the imposing figure of the Trojan prophetess, accusing her seducer Apollo:

Apollo! Apollo! God of the Gate, my Death-dealer! For thou hast destroyed me utterly, this second time! . . . Why then do I wear these mockeries of myself, this scepter, and these prophetic chaplets around my neck? I will destroy you before I meet my fate! Go, accursed that you are! . . . Go and enrich with doom another instead of me.

How often I have thought of these terrifying lines when contemplating the picture of my poor sister Camille, who died after thirty years' incarceration in the psychiatric hospital at Montfavet! And so many other poor creatures—Poe, Baudelaire, Nerval, and many, many more! It is the same with Phaedra. In vain she looks to an embrace as something human which may heal the ancient wound. Nothing can help her. In the last lines of the tragedy she turns toward us a face petrified with the same horror as made the face of Cassandra grow pale. My sister too, at the end of her conscious life, saw the face of the Gorgon reflected in the shield of Perseus. This is the *dénouement* of *Phèdre*. You know those incredible lines, which I cannot read without a shudder, in which, from the depths of Hell, she flings forth a despairing cry to that Father in Heaven from whom she has her being. It was right and natural that after writing them the pen should break of its own accord in the mighty hand that held it.

7 October 1954

Notes and References

PART I

[1] Paul Claudel, *Cahier Claudel 1* (Paris: N. R. F. edition, Librairie Gallimard, 1959), p. 93.

[2] Ibid., p. 105.

[3] Ibid., p. 107.

[4] Claudel, *Théâtre*, vol. 1 (Paris: N. R. F.–Pléiade edition, Librairie Gallimard, 1947), p. 676.

[5] Ibid., p. 252.

[6] Ibid., p. 271.

[7] Claudel, *Oeuvres poétiques* (Paris: N. R. F.–Pléiade edition, Librairie Gallimard, 1957), p. 39.

[8] Unpublished manuscript.

[9] From the *Programme* of the Théâtre de l'Oeuvre.

[10] Claudel, *Oeuvres complètes de Paul Claudel de L'Academie Française*, vol. 9 (Paris: N. R. F. edition, Librairies Gallimard, 1950).

[11] Ibid.

[12] From the *Programme* of the Théâtre de l'Oeuvre.

[13] These two anonymous articles are by Claudel. This is confirmed by his letters to Milhaud, Lugné-Poe, and Copeau.

[14] Translator's note: In the French edition of this book, the editors noted that this word was misprinted in the original as "ligne" (line), and they changed it to "lépre" (leprosy).

[15] Claudel, *Cahier Claudel 5.*

[16] Claudel, *Cahier Claudel 3*, pp. 36 ff.

[17] Claudel, *Cahier Claudel 6*, pp. 74 ff.

[18] These two letters were reprinted in Claudel, *Positions et Propositions 1* (Paris: Librairies Gallimard, 1959), under the title "Le Théâtre catholique."

[19] Claudel, *Oeuvres complètes*, vol. 18.

[20] This letter appeared in *Le Temps*, June 9, 1930. See *Oeuvres complètes*, vol. 10.

[21] Claudel, *Cahier Claudel 3*, pp. 66 ff.

[22] These notes on Nijinsky appear in *Positions et Propositions 1.*
[23] All these passages appeared in Claudel, *L'Oiseau noir dans de soleil levant* (Paris: Gallimard, 1929).
[24] Claudel, *Oeuvres complètes*, vol. 12, pp. 9–10, 86–90, 283–285.

PART II

[1] This text appears in all the French editions of *Sous le rempart d'Athènes.* We have given extracts.
[2] The following letters to Milhaud appeared in Claudel, *Cahier Claudel 3.*
[3] Milhaud, Darius. *Notes sans musique* (Paris: Julliard, 1949), pp. 237–238.
[4] The two "notes" were reprinted in Claudel, *Théâtre*, vol. 2 (Paris: Pléiade, 1966).
[5] This essay appears in French editions of *Le Livre de Christophe Colomb* as a preface.
[6] Claudel, *Cahier Claudel 3*, pp. 123 ff.
[7] Translator's note: These are simply the stage directions exactly as given in the edition of the play apart from the repetition of "trompettes." They can be translated as follows:
Bells in the distance, almost imperceptible.
Trumpets, trumpets, trumpets,
Trumpets in the distance.
The bells again, very clear.
Bells far away, less distinct.
[8] This lecture was printed for the first time in *Théâtre*, vol. 2.
[9] This note appears in all French editions of *L'Histoire de Tobie et de Sara.*
[10] Claudel, *Cahier Claudel 3.*
[11] This is an unpublished text which is among the documents of Louis Jouvet, in the form of handwritten and typed notes. We give the typed version, which we have edited.

PART III

[1] Claudel, *Oeuvres complètes*, vol. 12.
[2] René Viviani, *La Mission française en Amérique* (Paris: Flammarion, 1917).
[3] Text given in *Cahier de la compagnie Renaud-Barrault*, Year 1, No. 1. (Paris: Julliard, 1953).
[4] Claudel, *Oeuvres complètes*, vol. 12.
[5] Translator's note: Presumably Plutarch.
[6] Translator's note: P. P. C.: in French, "pour prendre conge" which in English is "to take leave."
[7] Claudel, *Oeuvres en prose* (Paris: N. R. F.–Pléiade edition), p. 436.
[8] Translator's note: "They don't simply happen" is in English in the original.
[9] Claudel, *Oeuvres complètes*, vol. 14.

[10] Translator's note: "Great St. James, bring back Christopher Columbus who has gone to get our money!"

[11] Translator's note: In English in the original.

[12] Claudel, *Oeuvres complètes*, vol. 11.

[13] Unpublished manuscript.

[14] Extracted from "La Poesie est un art," published in 1952, in *Oeuvres en prose*, p. 52.

[15] Claudel, *Memoires improvisés* (Paris: N. R. F. edition, Librairie Gallimard, 1954), p. 313 ff.

[16] Claudel, *Oeuvres en prose*, p. 479. Text dating from 1952.

[17] Claudel, *Memoires improvisés*, p. 149.

[18] Ibid., p. 33.

[19] Ibid., p. 36.

[20] Ibid., p. 318.

[21] Claudel, *Oeuvres en prose*, p. 448.

[22] Translator's note: This expression is in English in the original.

[23] Translator's note: "Forget it, Lord, and for all future time may eternal silence hide this memory."

[24] Translator's note: "Let us flee from this deep dreadful place where virtue breathes a poisoned air."

[25] Translator's note: "Salamis witnessing the tears of Periboea."

[26] Translator's note: "Ariadne reciting her wrongs to the rocks."

[27] Translator's note: "That, going down to Hell with Pirithoüs, he has seen Cocytus and the gloomy shores, and has shown himself, living, to the shades below."

[28] Translator's note: "Phaedra boasted in vain of Theseus' sighs. I am prouder, and I spurn the easy glory of snatching at a homage offered to a thousand others, and entering a heart that is open to everyone. But to sway an inflexible mind, to bring pain to an unfeeling soul, to chain a captive amazed at his fetters, struggling in vain against a yoke he loves. . . ."

[29] Translator's note: "To unfold its uncertain tangle."

[30] Translator's note: "I cannot look at myself without horror."

Index of the Principal Themes